C

HEALTH

Dr R.M. Youngson
with
The Diagram Group

HarperCollins*Publishers*

HarperCollins Publishers
P.O. Box, Glasgow G4 0NB

A Diagram book first created by Diagram Visual
Information Limited of 195 Kentish Town Road,
London NW5 8SY

First published 1995

Reprint 10 9 8 7 6 5 4 3 2 1 0

© Diagram Visual Information Limited 1995

ISBN 0 00 470642 0

All information given in this book has been fully checked
and approved by experienced medical staff. However, the
Collins *Gem Holiday Health* is not intended as a
substitute for professional medical care. It should only be
used as a guide to actions that may be needed prior to
obtaining appropriate professional treatment.

Printed in Great Britain by
HarperCollins Manufacturing, Glasgow

Introduction

More and more people are enjoying the pleasures of holidays abroad. With the pleasures of travel come potential pitfalls, however, especially regarding the traveller's health and well-being. In order to get the most out of your travel – whether a business trip or a holiday – it's wise to be prepared for the health risks you might encounter. Most health hazards can be avoided by taking reasonable precautions and behaving sensibly.

The *Collins Gem Holiday Health* provides the up-to-date information you need to prevent ill-health or injury from ruining your travels. In a clear, user-friendly format, it guides you through the steps you need to take before leaving, describes the potential dangers of heat and cold, insect bites and tropical diseases, and discusses how to prevent them or minimize their effect. It offers practical advice on what to do if you fall ill or are injured abroad – where to go for help, how medical treatment is provided in both European Economic Area (EEA) and non-EEA countries – and what to do when you return. The Helplines listed in the Appendix provide the names and addresses of useful travel health organizations and other details on resources for travellers.

Wherever your travels take you – to the British seaside or the deepest Amazon – the *Collins Gem Holiday Health* will prove to be an indispensable source of knowledge and information.

Contents

4. KEEPING SAFE

5. SEX AND THE TRAVELLER

6. DISEASE DIRECTORY

7. MEDICAL TREATMENT ABROAD

8. AFTER YOU RETURN

Special circumstances directory

PREGNANT TRAVELLERS

TRAVELLING WITH CHILDREN

1. Planning

CHECKLIST

Any journey, especially travel to tropical or poor countries where good medical services may not be readily available, needs planning well ahead. Answer 'yes' or 'no' to the questions below. If your answer is in red type – or you don't know what to answer – you need to make special preparations detailed in this chapter.

- Do you feel fit enough for a tiring journey by plane/car/bus/boat? **YES** NO
- Do you feel fit enough for a break from your normal routine, far away from your usual medical help? **YES** NO
- Do you know what the special health risks are at your destination? **YES** NO
- Are you protected against infectious diseases prevalent at your destination? **YES** NO
- Do you need to take any special precautions before travelling – e.g. vaccinations? YES **NO**
- Will you need to take regular medication while you are away? YES **NO**
- Are there restrictions on importing drugs into the country you are visiting? YES **NO**
- Do you know what to do if you become ill while you are away? **YES** NO
- Have you arranged travel insurance? **YES** NO

- Do you know what you need to include
  in your travel first aid kit?   **YES NO**
- Would you mind being treated in hospital
  by physicians who may not speak your
  language or understand your culture?   **YES NO**

FITNESS TESTS

Visit your doctor for a check-up before you go.
A heart malfunction, high blood pressure, or breathing
problems can be dangerous if you are travelling.
Essential health checks before you travel include
checking blood pressure and listening to the chest.

Certificates of fitness and doctor's notes

A note or certificate from your doctor could be very
useful in the circumstances listed below. Take several
photocopies of the note before leaving and give them to
medical staff abroad, keeping the original somewhere
safe.

- If you will be travelling by ship and are over age 75,
  you may be required to provide a fitness certificate.
- If you are pregnant, especially in your third
  trimester, you might need a note from your doctor
  confirming your expected date of delivery and your
  current state of general health. Most airlines will
  refuse to carry you if you are near your due date.
- If you are taking medication for any medical
  condition, have your doctor give you a note detailing
  the diagnosis and current treatment.
- If you take sleeping tablets, tranquillizers, or opioid
  painkillers you must get a note from your doctor
  stating that the drugs are for medical treatment and
  may be supplied to you.

- If you have kidney disease and require dialysis while abroad, a letter from your doctor should confirm your requirements. Plan this well in advance.

Remember, a long journey – even a holiday tour – disrupts your routine and your body clock. Plan to give yourself time for rest, recuperation, and exercise.

Fitness to drive

Consider your fitness to drive long distances abroad:

- If you are a hay fever sufferer, plan your driving trip for times of the year when the pollen count is likely to be lowest in the country you are visiting (see p. 66). Hay fever makes you feel tired, and most antihistamine drugs cause drowsiness.
- If you are asthmatic, minimize motorway driving and plan your route to bypass heavily industrialized regions and cities with poor air quality (check with motoring and environmental organizations).
- If you need glasses or contact lenses, take a spare pair in case of loss or damage.

YOU SHOULD NOT DRIVE:

- if you have had attacks of fainting or dizziness
- if you experience angina pains (an intense pain spreading outward from the mid-chest), or are being treated for angina or abnormal heartbeat – some of the drugs cause drowsiness
- if you have had a heart attack in the last two months
- if you have recently had a stroke
- if you have Ménière's disease
- for a year after a major skull fracture
- if you have the eye disorders diplopia or macular degeneration, or within two months of a cataract operation

If in doubt about your fitness to drive, consult your doctor first.

There are fewer things to consider when assessing your fitness to be a passenger rather than a driver, but bear in mind that long periods of sitting can put a strain on the veins in the legs and on the back and bottom.

Fitness to fly

Flying may be dangerous if you suffer from any of the following conditions:

- lung problems causing breathlessness at rest (e.g. emphysema, severe chronic bronchitis, bronchiectasis), or collapse of a lung or recent removal of a lung
- severe anaemia (shortage of haemoglobin)
- heart problems (e.g. heart failure, unstable angina pectoris, a heart attack in the past month or severe atherosclerosis)
- recent surgery (to the chest, abdomen, ear or within the skull)
- circulatory problems, including deep vein thrombosis or pulmonary embolism
- third-trimester pregnancy (risk of starting labour)
- severe diabetes
- acute anxiety disorders, a tendency to hyperventilate when anxious or any psychiatric disorder involving violent behaviour

If you have one of these conditions and you decide to fly, or if you have any special needs such as wheelchair access, inform the airline well in advance so the necessary arrangements can be made.

In addition, the following conditions can cause discomfort while flying:

- head cold with blocked eustachian tubes
- sinus trouble
- colostomy (can cause excess gas production)
- fractures with long plaster or plastic casts, or fractured, wired jaw

If in doubt about your fitness to fly, consult your doctor.

Fitness to travel by ship

Most large passenger liners have adequate, and often excellent, medical facilities. Because of the isolation from specialist medical services, however, the threat of serious illness at sea is always a matter of concern. If you have a history of a significant and persisting medical condition, get a full report from your doctor before you travel. Large liners carry reasonable stocks of important drugs, but you must not rely on this for supplies; take an adequate supply of any medication you are on.

If you have a serious medical condition, do not voyage on the cheap. The medical facilities and quality care on board some package holiday ships may be minimal, so check before you book. Bring seasickness remedies with you (see p.36).

Some medical conditions are of special relevance for sea travellers. These include:

- any disorder known to be liable to progress rapidly
- 'grumbling' appendix (risk of acute flare-up requiring surgery)
- severe peptic ulceration (risk of perforation or severe bleeding requiring surgery)
- oesophageal varices (risk of dangerous bleeding)

- unstable angina pectoris (risk of heart attack)
- severe asthma (risk of uncontrollable spasm of the bronchii)

If in doubt about your fitness to travel by ship, consult your doctor first.

PREGNANT TRAVELLERS

Travelling does not harm pregnant women or their unborn babies (see p.22 for immunization). However, it is worth remembering that:

- pregnancy is unpredictable. You should not travel where you cannot rely on first-class medical care.
- during the first three months of pregnancy there is a risk of miscarriage or discovery of an ectopic pregnancy (in which the embryo develops in a Fallopian tube), and consequent haemorrhage. This risk increases if you are pregnant for the first time or if you have a history of miscarriage.
- during the last three months of pregnancy there is an increased danger of complications, possibly requiring highly sophisticated treatment
- there is a risk of starting labour if you fly during late pregnancy. Most airlines will not carry passengers who are more than 32 weeks pregnant.
- fatigue is very common, especially in late pregnancy. Plan your itinerary accordingly. Organise a day for rest after your journey, and allow for short periods of activity (e.g. for sightseeing excursions).

Medical insurance

Complications in pregnancy may require expensive

hospital treatment. Medical insurance covering pregnancy is essential, but premiums are high.

DO STATE ON YOUR PERSONAL MEDICAL FACT SHEET (see pp.28–9) THAT YOU ARE PREGNANT.

TRAVELLING WITH CHILDREN

There is obviously much more preparation involved when travelling with children, especially babies.

- For older children, you will need a supply of toys and books for the journey.
- For babies – depending on your destination – you may need to bring a supply of disposable nappies for the duration of the trip; they may be hard to get and are likely to be expensive. If you bottle feed, pack enough formula milk for the trip. Premixed formula is easier and removes the necessity of using boiled or bottled water for feeds, but it is heavy and is only suitable for shorter trips.
- If you are flying with a baby under about nine months old, arrange beforehand for a cot (called a 'bassinet') to be supplied by the airline. This is usually simply a cardboard box which you can place on the floor in front of you. Most airlines will also have nappies and a limited supply of baby food on board. You may be able to get a special child's meal, but request it when you book.

Other items that may be needed when travelling with babies and small children include:

- high-factor suncream and hats
- travel sickness medicine – e.g. Phenergan

- lightweight fold-up pushchair
- front or back baby carrier
- infant car seat if you're hiring a car

(See also medical kits, pp.30–1).

Preliminary health precautions

Do not travel with babies under a month old, especially to areas where good medical care is not available. Babies need careful monitoring in the first weeks of life. Newborn babies under two days old may not have fully expanded lungs and may be at risk from lowered oxygen levels in aircraft.

See pp.22–3 for more information on immunization for children, and p.58 for more information on disease prevention in children.

TRAVELLERS WITH SPECIAL CIRCUMSTANCES

Careful planning and thorough preparation are keys to successful travel for people whose mobility is impaired, who are blind or deaf, or who have a medical condition that requires special medication or other treatment.

- Travel within the EU, North America, Australia and New Zealand, and other industrialized countries is becoming easier for people with special needs.
- If you plan to travel to eastern Europe, Africa, Asia or South America it is best to book a trip with a group to be sure that the facilities you need will be provided and that you can travel in comfort. It would be unwise to venture far outside the major cities of Africa, for example, without prearranged private transport. Public transport tends to be crowded to

bursting point and unreliable, roads may be poor, and modern hotels and medical facilities may be scarce.

- If you are not travelling with a group, start planning your trip some months in advance.
- Wheelchair access will be easiest in modern international hotels, which also have porters, medical facilities, menus for special diets, and other services.
- If you need special medical care, find out about the medical facilities available and be sure they are adequate to deal fully with your condition.

Medication

If you are on medication for any condition, it would be sensible to get a note from your doctor detailing the diagnosis and current treatment. Also, check whether you will be crossing time zones (see pp.46–7), and adjust the timing of the medication as necessary. (Also, see p.19 on taking drugs abroad.)

Restricted mobility

Airlines now need only be notified, on booking, of the need for wheelchair access. You may be asked to get to the airport early so that you can board and be settled before the other passengers. Lightweight folding wheelchairs that can be stowed away during the journey are best for air travel. Consider well in advance how to overcome the problem of getting into the lavatory on board an aircraft (airports have washrooms with wide doors and ramps).

- When booking, tell the clerk if your wheelchair is battery driven, since the carriage of batteries is restricted for security reasons.

Blindness

Guide dogs are accepted in aircraft, but check with the
consulate of your destination country whether there is a
quarantine period or if there are other regulations
regarding taking dogs into the country you plan to visit.
Bear in mind the risk of rabies in many countries and
consider managing without your dog. Group trips and
tours are a safe alternative.

Diabetes

It may be unwise to travel by air if you are severely
diabetic and suffer from airsickness, since you risk
losing diabetic control. Long travel delays may also
delay mealtimes. Sea travel is a better method of travel,
since ocean liners carry a ship's doctor and refrigeration
facilities, and there is little danger of having to skip a
meal. You should alert the shipping company to the fact
that you are diabetic. If you have a MedicAlert
medallion, wear this at all times.

Long-distance road travel needs to be well planned to
ensure that you can get regular meals and adequate
daily exercise. Refrigeration of insulin will be a
constant problem if you are travelling by car or coach
in hot areas. If the condition is causing arterial
complications, plan only short sightseeing trips on foot,
as walking may be uncomfortable.

Heart and circulatory conditions

If you have a heart or circulatory condition, you should
avoid the high-altitude destinations where breathing
might be difficult. Check the prevailing temperatures at
the time of year you want to travel, and avoid very cold

places. You might also avoid hilly towns and resorts, where you would have to walk up steep hills for much of the time. Walking is excellent exercise, but it must not put excessive strain on the heart.

Kidney disease

Kidney patients who need regular dialysis will need a doctor's help in arranging dialysis at centres in the country they plan to visit.

TAKING DRUGS ABROAD

Customs authorities are sensitive to the movement of drugs of any kind across international frontiers. Control of the movement of a number of drugs is the subject of international treaty agreements, and some countries regard as a criminal offence the importation of any drug that might be regarded as a drug of abuse or a potential drug of abuse. For these reasons, you should be careful to carry with you only drugs that are necessary and that have been prescribed for you by a doctor. Don't even consider carrying across frontiers any of the common drugs of addiction or abuse, such as heroin, cocaine, crack cocaine, marijuana or LSD. In some countries the death penalty is used against those who do.

CARRIAGE OF DRUGS
If in doubt about possible restrictions on the carriage of drugs out of or into the UK or the country you are visiting, call the Home Office Drugs Branch to get expert advice (tel. 071 273 3806).

DRUGS FOR WHICH YOU NEED A DOCTOR'S CERTIFICATE

Many prescription drugs have psychoactive (i.e. mood changing) properties and can readily be abused. If you have to carry any of these drugs, obtain a note from your doctor certifying that they have been prescribed and are necessary for medical treatment. If you must obtain these while travelling, also carry a letter to a doctor in the country you are visiting requesting that the necessary drugs be supplied.

The following are psychoactive drugs:

- major painkilling drugs, especially of the opioid group – e.g. DF 118
- any tranquillizing drug – e.g. Valium
- drugs containing amphetamine or one of the amphetamine-like substances. This group includes several drugs used for weight control – e.g. Ponderax.
- barbiturate drugs, including those used for epilepsy control – e.g. Phenobarbitone.

Antimalarial drugs

One of the most important health risks in the tropics is malaria (see pp.172–6). This potentially serious disease occurs in more than 100 countries, especially certain countries in Africa, South America, the Indian subcontinent, the Middle East, the Far East and parts of China. You can get almost complete protection against malaria by taking certain drugs before you travel, during your stay, and after your return. If you are going to a malarial area, get supplies of the preventive drug in good time. See your doctor about this as soon as possible. There is more about malaria in Chapter 6.

Non-prescription drugs

Travelling with over-the-counter preparations (for example, paracetamol or travel sickness medicine) is not restricted. A list of which non-prescription medications to take is included on pp.30–1 in the Traveller's Medical Kit. Although many of these are available abroad, it is wise (and in some cases less expensive) to obtain them before you travel.

Packaging

To avoid any problems with authorities when taking drugs abroad, make sure all medicines (both prescription and over-the-counter) are accurately labelled and kept in their original containers. Keep out of direct sunlight – heat can damage their effectiveness.

IMMUNIZATION

There are certain diseases against which you should be immunized, whether you plan to travel or not. This is the advice of the Department of Health. Your immunization should have been done during childhood and adolescence, to be protected against:

- diphtheria
- whooping cough
- mumps
- tetanus
- polio
- measles
- German measles (rubella; females only at present)
- tuberculosis (with BCG)

If you are an adult and think you might not have been immunized against any of these, you will probably have acquired immunity naturally against most of them except polio, tetanus and diphtheria. You should certainly get yourself protected against these.

IMMUNIZATION FOR SPECIAL CIRCUMSTANCES

PREGNANT TRAVELLERS

Some vaccines can harm an embryo or early fetus. These include:

- diphtheria
- tuberculosis (BCG vaccine)
- measles
- rubella (German measles)
- polio
- typhoid
- yellow fever

See pp.24–5 for more information on immunization generally, and Chapter 6 for more on immunization for specific diseases

BABIES AND CHILDREN

Babies under six months should not be immunized against cholera, yellow fever, typhoid, hepatitis A or rabies. In the few countries where a yellow fever vaccination certificate is required, they are exempt.

Children under one year are not normally given cholera or typhoid injections.

Children are especially susceptible to:

Hepatitis A This is a liver infection spread by faecal contamination of food and water. It occurs where hygiene is poor, especially in food preparation. Gamma globulin injections give short-term protection, but may be painful. A course of injections with a new vaccine gives long-term protection, but you have to pay.

Malaria Children of any age should take antimalarial tablets in a dosage carefully adjusted according to weight. Consult your doctor. They should also wear clothes covering their legs and arms at dawn and dusk and sleep under a mosquito net.

Measles In some poor countries this is a serious disease. Healthy children are unlikely to be badly affected, but you should check whether immunization is necessary for the area you are visiting.

Meningitis This infection of the brain coverings occurs almost everywhere, but is prevalent in parts of Africa and Asia. Watch for symptoms (see pp.178–80). It responds to antibiotics.

Meningococcal meningitis Also called cerebrospinal fever or spotted fever (see pp.178–80), this disease tends to occur in epidemics, and affects children more than adults. Children over six months should be immunized if visiting a high risk area.

Tetanus Newborn babies are susceptible to infection through the stump of the umbilical cord. All children should be immunized or given an anti-tetanus booster from two months.

Tuberculosis All children, including newborn babies, travelling to areas where tuberculosis is prevalent should be immunized against it (see pp.190–1).

See Chapter 6 for more information on specific diseases.

Minimum ages for vaccination

Age	Vaccination	Boosters
2 months	diphtheria tetanus polio	before starting school and at 15–19 years
	whooping cough	none
over 6 months	all vaccinations available to adults (except typhoid and cholera injections)	
1 year	cholera typhoid	

OLDER TRAVELLERS

If you are over 60 and suffering from diabetes, heart, lung or kidney disease, or if you are having treatment that affects your immune system, you should be immunized against flu (influenza). Typhoid affects elderly people seriously and can cause death. You should be vaccinated if you are over 60

HIV-POSITIVE TRAVELLERS

Whether you have symptoms or not, if you are being immunized against measles, mumps, rubella, and polio you should not have live vaccines. For whooping cough, tetanus, diphtheria, typhoid, cholera, and hepatitis B you should have inactivated vaccines. Yellow fever vaccine may be unsafe; ask your doctor. BCG should not be given.

How immunization works

Immunization works by activating the body's own natural defences against disease. Protective vaccines can be given by tablet, injection or even a scratch on the skin. Boosters are additional doses of the vaccine given later to ensure continuing protection.

Protection for travellers

Few countries now refuse entry to visitors on the grounds of lack of immunization protection except when epidemics occur; yellow fever is the only disease for which immunization is required for entry to some countries.

Remember that when travelling, particularly outside Europe and North America, your body will be exposed to diseases against which you have no natural immunity.

- Don't neglect immunization. Check the Helplines (pp.245–7) to see if you need it where you're going.
- Find out about immunization two or three months before you travel; some jabs are needed well in advance of your departure date.
- Check with your own doctor about the likely effect of immunization on any special condition you already have (see Immunization for special circumstances, pp.22–3).
- There is no vaccine against malaria, but there is an effective course of drug treatment you should follow.
- Chapter 6 lists some of the most dangerous diseases in the world, and describes how to protect yourself from them. Many diseases occur only in specific regions of a country; travelling outside those regions

will not put you at risk of contracting the disease. It is therefore important to check with your doctor or with one of the organizations listed in Helplines, pp.245–7, to determine if immunization is advisable for your particular destination.

Don't worry unnecessarily: remember that fit and well-prepared travellers are seldom at risk. Immunization and taking sensible precautions are the most effective preventive measures.

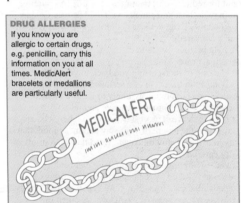

DRUG ALLERGIES
If you know you are allergic to certain drugs, e.g. penicillin, carry this information on you at all times. MedicAlert bracelets or medallions are particularly useful.

MEDICAL INSURANCE

Never underestimate the costs of an illness or injury
while abroad. Medical costs can be ruinous; you could
be liable for hundreds of thousands of pounds for major
treatment. For minor illnesses, especially in areas with
high medical costs, patients who cannot pay may be
turned away. Medical cover is essential.

You are likely to be covered for emergency medical
attention within the European Economic Area (EEA),
and for reduced-cost treatment in non-EEA countries
with reciprocal agreements with the UK (see Chapter 7
for details). Even in these countries, however, you will
not be covered for:

- long periods of health care
- private care
- the cost of transporting you back to your home
  country in the event of a serious illness or injury.

Unless you are obviously likely to require medical
treatment while abroad, adequate and reliable insurance
is not expensive. The cost depends on where you are
travelling, the length of your stay and the amount that is
covered. Don't stint on cover. Read the small print
very carefully.

If you are driving, investigate the travel health
insurance offered by the international motoring
organizations; their plans include repatriation of you,
your vehicle and passengers if you are taken ill.

Other points to consider include the following:

- If you are travelling to areas near the borders with
  other countries, obtain cover for all countries. You
  could be taken to another country in an emergency.
- Check the payment policy. Will the insurers pay the

costs direct or must you pay, and be reimbursed at the end of treatment?

- Check arrangements for obtaining money quickly if you are expected to pay for your treatment and be reimbursed later.
- Does the policy cover air ambulance, if necessary?
- Does the policy exclude cover for an existing condition? If so, you can negotiate a premium so that it is included as well.
- Does the policy cover injuries in certain named sports?
- Are special winter sports covered (e.g. skiing)?
- Does the policy cover infants up to age two?
- Is the premium higher for travellers over age 70? (If so, you might find a better deal by shopping around.)
- Is lost or stolen luggage covered? Many policies automatically include this. If you don't want it, you might be able to negotiate a reduction in the premium.
- Obtain a 24-hour telephone number where you can reach the insurer to get information.

A GOOD POLICY SHOULD COVER:

- consultation and treatment by a doctor or at a clinic if you suffer from a minor illness
- the cost of an ambulance and emergency treatment in hospital if you have an accident or severe illness
- the cost of surgery if you need an operation
- the cost of transportation if you are repatriated
- rapid payment, or reimbursement of the money if you have to pay for treatment

Note that these are minimum requirements; most policies should cover much more.

PERSONAL MEDICAL CARD

Create your own personal fact sheet, including your
medical details, and carry it with you. Leave a
photocopy with friends or relatives. Include the
following details:

Names and addresses

- your name
- your date of birth
- your home address
- your home telephone number
- your work address
- your work telephone number
- name of your spouse or nearest relative
- contact telephone number of spouse or close relative
- names of your children/parents
- their contact telephone numbers
- name and address of your doctor

Medical

- your blood type if you know it (include Rh factor)
- list of the diseases you have had in the past
- allergies (penicillin, drugs, insect bites, etc.)
- dates of most recent immunizations including:
    - tetanus
    - measles
    - diphtheria
    - polio
    - other

- if you are pregnant, relevant details and expected
  delivery date

- any present medical conditions (asthma, epilepsy, diabetes, etc.)
- list any medicines taken regularly (state the name of the medicine, the reason for it being taken, dose and how often you take it)
- a note of any special precautions or other information that might be relevant (e.g. whether you have a pacemaker)

Insurance details

- name, address and contact telephone number of your insurance company
- policy number for your car if relevant
- policy number for life insurance and accidents

Personal Medical Fact Sheet

MICHAEL ROBERT JONES

Date of birth: 23/6/62
Home address: 236 Perth Road, Sevenoaks, Kent, England, UK
Home telephone no: (0972) 66713
Work telephone no: (071) 897765
Parent's address: 425B Mill Lane, Redhill, Surrey, England, UK
Parent's telephone no: (0807) 33719
Doctor: Dr. D. G. Small;
Windmill Road Surgery, Sevenoaks, Kent. (0972) 61735

MEDICAL HISTORY

Blood type: A⁺
Previous illnesses: German measles (1971); Hepatitis A (1982)
Allergies: Wasp stings; Amoxycillin
Recent immunizations: Tetanus (1992); Polio (1989); Yellow fever (1991)
Asthma

TRAVELLER'S MEDICAL KIT

A GENERAL MEDICAL KIT FOR TRAVELLING ABROAD

Tablets
Headache, indigestion, travel sickness, diarrhoea. Also, laxatives, anti-worm tablets, antibiotics (a doctor's prescription is needed), aspirin, paracetamol, water purification (depending on where you are travelling), hay fever, antihistamine (for severe bites)

Lotions
Antiseptic, calamine lotion (for sunburn), sunscreen, antifungal powder, insect repellents

Dressings
Plasters, sterile wound dressings, bandages, steristrips, adhesive tape, cotton wool

Utility items
Safety pins, scissors, tweezers, sterile needles, thermometer

Miscellaneous
Nasal spray, cold symptom remedy, eye lotion/drops, contact lens solutions

ADDITIONS TO MEDICAL KITS

For children

- rehydrating fluids or powder
- children's paracetamol (for fever and pain relief)
- travel sickness elixir
- high-factor sunscreen
- sunburn lotion
- insect repellent (spray or solid)
- teething gel

For women

- cystitis treatment
- treatment for thrush
- tampons/pads

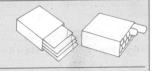

For men and women

- birth control

Anti-AIDS/hepatitis kit

- sterile syringes
- sterile needles
- condoms

(Kits can be purchased ready-made; see Helplines, pp.245–7.)

2. Travelling

STRESS REDUCTION

Whatever your state of health, the prospect of a journey is usually an exciting and pleasurable one. But travel itself can be stressful, especially if you are delayed at ports or airports. This stress can sometimes tip the balance from a pleasant experience into an ordeal. For this reason, whatever your method of travel, it is sensible to lead a normal life for the day or two prior departure, and to make your arrangements in plenty of time so as to avoid a last-minute rush.

Checklist

- Start preparing for the trip as far in advance as you can. Arrange relaxed schedules for vaccinations (see pp.21–5), and apply early for necessary documents.
- As the departure date approaches, draw up a daily timetable of things to do, and follow it.
- Pack as much as you can a day or two before the departure date, leaving yourself as little as possible to do on the day.
- On the day before departure, write a final list of things you will have to do on the day you leave.
- Get a good night's sleep the night before you travel.
- Practise the exercises opposite to relieve stress.

DRINKING ALCOHOL WHILE TRAVELLING

It's easy to drink too much while travelling. Drinks tend to be cheap and readily available, you're relaxed and on holiday, and everyday worries can be forgotten.
But remember that alcohol can remove inhibitions,

DEALING WITH STRESS

Deep-breathing exercise

1 Sit comfortably. Inhale slowly. Feel the air fill your lungs slowly from the bottom up.
2 Exhale slowly, relaxing as the air is expelled.
3 Concentrate on breathing in and out as slowly and as deeply as possible. Repeat ten times.

Three exercises to release tension from muscles

● Stretch your arms above your head (**a**); reach to the sky; hold for five seconds; relax. Repeat five times.
● Let your head rest to one side (**b**). Take a deep breath in and, as you exhale, concentrate on trying to let your ear relax to touch your shoulder. Repeat slowly five times, then repeat on the other side.
● Sit comfortably and lift your heels from the floor (**c**). Hold the position for five seconds, then relax (**d**). Repeat five times.

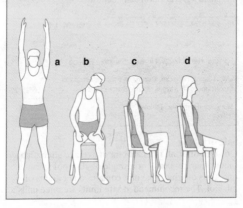

anxiety and a sense of responsibility. After too much to
drink, it's easy to get involved in sexual activity, with
its attendant risks of unplanned pregnancy and AIDS.
If you have a tendency to drink too much at home, this
may be exaggerated on holiday. For anyone on the
brink of an alcohol problem, a boozy trip can be a
nightmare. Seek help before you travel.

The effects of alcohol are enhanced by flying, and this
can leave you very dehydrated. Drink less alcohol on
planes and more water or fruit juices.

If you'll be driving while on holiday, remember that
many countries have stricter drink-drive laws than
Britain and that in some places random breath tests are
the norm. The box below compares the legal limits for
drivers in several European countries.

MAXIMUM PERMITTED BLOOD ALCOHOL LEVEL:	
Bulgaria, Poland	0.02%
Finland, Netherlands, Norway, Sweden, Greece	0.05%
UK, Austria, Belgium, Denmark, France, Germany, Luxembourg, Portugal, Spain, Switzerland	0.08%
Hungary, Romania, Turkey	no limit

Safe drinking

One unit of drink is a half-pint of average-strength beer
(about four per cent), or a single of 70-proof spirit, or
one glass of wine. One unit contains eight grams of
ethanol. The recommended safe limits are three units a

day for a woman, four for a man. It won't do any harm
if you exceed these a little while on holiday, but get
back to normal limits as soon as you can. Try to space
your drinks over time, drink only with food, and have a
glass of water with every alcoholic drink.

TRAVEL SICKNESS

Travel sickness is caused by abnormal stimulation of
the ear and other mechanisms that inform the brain of
the orientation of the head.

Air sickness is comparatively uncommon because most
planes fly too high for the worst turbulence. Occasional
bumpy episodes seldom last long. But for those who've
experienced sickness at sea or in cars, the symptoms are
distressingly familiar:

- dizziness
- nausea
- pale, clammy skin
- vomiting
- sweating of the face and hands

Symptoms may persist for several hours after the trip
has ended, with variable severity.

Travel sickness in children Get advice from a doctor
or pharmacist about the most appropriate travel
sickness medicine for babies and children. Hyoscine
drugs (e.g. Kwells) or a mild sedative such as that in
Phenergan are suitable for children, but be careful not
to give too large a dose or to repeat the dose too
frequently. Some drugs have undesirable side effects,
including dry mouth, blurred vision and drowsiness.

Pregnant travellers Most antihistamine and hyoscine pills are safe in pregnancy (check with your doctor), but do not take them if you are driving. They cause drowsiness and impair concentration and reaction time.

RELIEVING TRAVEL SICKNESS

- Fix your eyes on something static.
- Do not read.
- Avoid greasy or spicy food before or during travel.
- Avoid alcohol.
- Avoid other passengers who are also feeling sick.

Drugs for preventing travel sickness

The following are meant to be taken *before* travelling to prevent the onset of travel sickness. The time in which they take effect varies; follow instructions for the specific drug.

- hyoscine (e.g. Kwells)
- cyclizine (e.g. Marzine)
- promethazine (e.g. Phenergan, Avomine)
- dimenhydrinate (e.g. Dramamine)

The drug hyoscine is also available in the form of a patch that can be stuck behind the ear so that the drug is gradually absorbed into the bloodstream.

Drugs for relieving travel sickness

Once vomiting has started, hyoscine can be absorbed more quickly into the bloodstream by dissolving tablets in the mouth rather than swallowing them. Alternatively, if you are travelling on a ship with full medical facilities, a doctor may give an injection of an antihistamine drug or may prescribe such a drug in the form of a suppository. In very severe cases various powerful antiemetic drugs, such as metoclopramide (Maxolon) or ondansetron (Zofran) might be prescribed by a doctor.

AIR TRAVEL

Preparation

If you can, plan your flight time to take into account the effects of jet lag (see pp.45–8). If you have any dietary restrictions or special needs, tell the airline staff when you book; they will order special meals (e.g. low-salt, low-fat, vegetarian, kosher) to be provided during the flight.

Pre-flight anxiety

Organized preparation for a flight will help reduce the stress many people associate with flying.

- Start out early for the airport in case of traffic delays on the way so that you have plenty of time for formalities.
- On the day of departure, get up early and have a good breakfast.
- Before leaving the house, run through your day-of-the-flight checklist. Reassure yourself that water and gas taps and electrical appliances are switched off; that all alarms are on; and that the doors are securely locked.
- If you have to wait at the airport, try to rest. Occupy yourself with a book, conversation, a newspaper, or listening to a favourite tape.
- Try to avoid caffeinated coffee or alcohol while you wait. These can increase any anxiety you feel.
- Children usually enjoy flying, but they too can get stressed by delays. Take a supply of books, tapes and toys to keep them busy.

Airport medical services

With thousands of passengers passing through daily,
medical staff at large international airports have to deal
with serious illnesses, such as coronaries and strokes, as
well as premature births and minor accidents. Many
passengers become tense, nervous and accident-prone
at airports, develop headaches, migraine, and toothache
and suffer a number of minor injuries.

Civil Aviation Authority regulations stipulate that all
airports must arrange for local doctors and hospitals to
be on 24-hour emergency call, so if you are taken ill
while in transit you are assured of emergency medical
help. In addition, the largest airports have highly
sophisticated medical facilities, including 24-hour
services, with a full staff of doctors and nurses,
vaccination facilities and operating theatres.

These medical centres can handle large numbers of
passengers at a time. Some make charges for treatment;
others, such as Heathrow's services, give free
treatment. They deal, variously, with:

- airport emergencies and disasters
- medical screening of immigrant passengers
- vaccination of travellers abroad
- routine medical treatment of airline flight crews
- medical treatment of passengers

Aircraft medical facilities

All aircraft cabin crew have first-aid training and can
deal with medical emergencies, including emergency
births and asthma attacks, as well as minor accidents.
They can give you painkillers and remedies for colds

and flu. All aircraft carry well-stocked first-aid kits, oxygen, and some medicines.

Cabin staff are not medically qualified, however, and cannot be expected to make the best decisions about what to do in a serious medical emergency. The essential decision that must be made in the case of serious illness is whether to divert the flight or return to base, so as to obtain the quickest necessary medical treatment. This decision rests with the aircraft captain.

Fear of flying

This is a real phenomenon, especially for infrequent travellers. Many people will admit to some anxiety about flying, especially during take-off and landing. There are some people, however, for whom the fear of flying is a phobia. These people will show signs of severe anxiety (see box). People who react in this way to the thought of flying should discuss the matter with their doctors well in advance. Much can be done to reduce anxiety by using minor tranquillizers for a few days before and during the flight.

If you are taking tranquillizers, do not forget that their effect will be considerably enhanced by alcohol. The

---

SIGNS OF SEVERE ANXIETY

- muscle tension
- restlessness
- shakiness or trembling
- breathlessness and sometimes hyperventilation
- fast pulse
- dry mouth
- sweating hands
- irritability
- husky voice
- pallor
- dilated nostrils

combination might lead to your being fast asleep during the flight, and this might give you further cause for anxiety – problems with your ears or sinuses during descent, for example.

Emergencies

If you are at all nervous about flying, remind yourself that it is a far safer method of transport than road travel. All aircraft emergencies are carefully documented and investigated, and airline safety records are compiled and published.

Once on board:

- After boarding, read the safety instruction card and watch the demonstration of emergency procedures carefully.
- Locate the nearest emergency exit door and be sure you understand the evacuation procedure.
- Work out how to fasten and unfasten your seat belt quickly.
- Avoid too much alcohol before or during the flight.

DEALING WITH AN EMERGENCY IN FLIGHT

- If an emergency occurs, keep calm, watch the nearest flight attendant closely, and do exactly what he or she tells you to do.
- Take off your shoes if they have high, thin or wedge heels.
- If there is a fire, crawl toward an exit, keeping as close to the floor as possible.
- When you are told to exit, leave everything behind and move fast. Rapid exit is the key to survival.
- Get as far away from the aircraft as you can as soon as you get out.

Cabin pressure

Oxygen Aircraft fly at an altitude at which the atmospheric pressure is too low to sustain life. The air in the cabin must therefore be kept at a much higher pressure than the air outside. In practice, cabin pressure is usually kept at about the same pressure as the atmosphere at 1829 meters (6000 feet). This is about 600 mm of mercury pressure, somewhat less than the average pressure at sea level (760 mm Hg).

For most people, the difference is negligible and is unnoticed, but it does mean that cabin air contains less oxygen than the air near the ground. Oxygen is the most basic and vital requirement of the body. To anyone on the borderline of getting enough oxygen into the blood, and hence into the tissues, this difference can be dangerous. This includes anyone with certain medical conditions (see the conditions listed on p.12) as well as smokers and drinkers. You get a good oxygen supply only if:

- your lungs are able to pass oxygen adequately into your blood
- your blood contains normal quantities of the oxygen-carrying material haemoglobin
- your heart is working normally to convey the

SIGNS OF OXYGEN DEPRIVATION (HYPOXIA)

- euphoria
- impaired judgement and memory
- loss of coordination
- blue lips, ear lobes and nails

In cases of suspected hypoxia, airline staff will administer oxygen.

oxygenated blood round your body
- your arteries are wide enough to allow blood to pass to the tissues (especially the heart and brain) in adequate amounts

Ear problems Nearly everyone experiences some slight ear discomfort with the changes in atmospheric cabin pressure that occur as the aircraft passes rapidly from low to high altitudes and vice versa. In most people the problem solves itself automatically by a harmless and spontaneous 'popping' of the ears. You might also take boiled sweets with you to suck during take-off and landing, especially for any children travelling with you. Ear discomfort in babies can be prevented by crying or sucking – using a dummy or breast- or bottle-feeding, for instance.

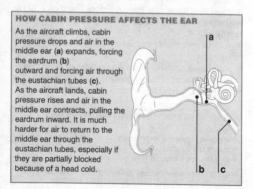

HOW CABIN PRESSURE AFFECTS THE EAR

As the aircraft climbs, cabin pressure drops and air in the middle ear (a) expands, forcing the eardrum (b) outward and forcing air through the eustachian tubes (c). As the aircraft lands, cabin pressure rises and air in the middle ear contracts, pulling the eardrum inward. It is much harder for air to return to the middle ear through the eustachian tubes, especially if they are partially blocked because of a head cold.

Sinus problems The sinuses are membrane-lined air cavities in the bones of the skull around the nose. They connect with the nose by means of short tubes also lined with mucous membrane. If this membrane is inflamed and swollen – if you have a cold, for instance – the high-pressure air may be able to force itself out during the ascent of the aircraft, but the chances are that the air will not be able to get back as the atmospheric pressure rises on the descent of the aircraft. The result may be severe sinus pain. This is not dangerous, but can be very uncomfortable. Nasal sprays or drops might help.

RELIEVING PRESSURE AGAINST THE EARDRUM

If you do not experience your ears 'popping', it is usually a simple matter to equalize the air pressure on the two sides of the eardrums. Try frequent swallowing, faking a big yawn or moving your jaw from side to side. Alternatively, suck a boiled sweet if you have one. This will usually relieve the discomfort. If this does not work, try the following:

1 Pinch your nostrils shut.
2 Breathe in through your mouth.
3 Shut your mouth.
4 Compress the air in your mouth and nose
   by trying to breathe out.

Do this as the plane climbs to flying altitude. Repeat if you have discomfort or if your hearing acuity diminishes. Then repeat as the plane descends.

If you have a cold or sinusitis, you'll probably feel greater pressure in your ears while flying. Use a nasal decongestant spray or drops.

Stomach problems The drop in cabin pressure at
cruising altitude – usually equal to the outside pressure
at about 1829 m – can have a surprising effect on your
stomach. We all have some gas in our intestines, and
the movement of gas within it is often audible. As the
cabin pressure drops, this gas expands greatly and the
normal intestinal 'milking' contractions (peristalsis) can
become even more audible. Most distressing of all is
when the expanding gas reaches the rectum and
balloons it out. This ballooning is only too apparent to
the sufferer and the need to release the pressure may
become irresistible.

One way to minimize the discomfort is to avoid gas-
inducing foods (such as beans) and fizzy drinks before
and during the flight. You will also find loose-fitting
clothes much more comfortable than tight garments.

Leg swelling

Sitting in cramped conditions with little leg room for
hours on end can cause swollen legs and feet in some
people. This is caused by an impeded blood flow in the
body; partial stagnation of blood in the feet and ankles
leads to waterlogging of the tissues (oedema). The most
obvious effect of oedema is that your shoes feel tight
and uncomfortable. If you are otherwise healthy,
oedema is, in itself, of little consequence and will soon
disappear once your journey is over.

If you suffer from problem veins you will be more
prone to thrombophlebitis (vein swelling and clot
formation) or the potentially dangerous deep vein
thrombosis (DVT). DVT can lead to pulmonary
embolism in which a blood clot breaks loose from the

vein, is carried to the heart and then to the lungs where it blocks the main blood access vessels. This can be fatal. Fortunately, preventive and relief measures are easy and straightforward.

RELIEVING LEG SWELLING
- Sit so that you minimize pressure on the backs of your legs.
- Keep your legs uncrossed while sitting.
- Put your feet up using carry-on baggage to take the pressure off the backs of your thighs.
- Move your feet regularly, and wiggle your toes.
- Contract your calf muscles.
- Get up and walk at regular intervals.
- Wear flat, comfortable shoes.

Jet lag

Your internal body clock is normally set to your local time. If you move rapidly by air across time zones, your body rhythms and the biochemical and physiological processes associated with them are temporarily 'out of sync' with local time.

The problem is always worse on an eastward journey when you must, in effect, shorten your day, and less troublesome when going west. This is partly because the body's internal rhythm is on a roughly 24-hour cycle. When crossing several time zones, the external 'day' is increasingly shorter or longer than 24 hours, disrupting the body's normal rhythm. The effects of jet lag will also be increased by lack of sleep during the flight. A jet-lagged person is:

- wakeful during the night and sleepy during the day
- liable to want to pass water during the night

TIME ZONES AROUND THE WORLD

Some countries, including the UK, adopt Daylight Saving Time (DST) in order to receive more daylight in summer. Clocks are

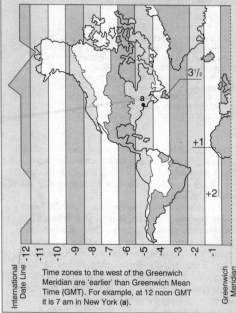

Time zones to the west of the Greenwich Meridian are 'earlier' than Greenwich Mean Time (GMT). For example, at 12 noon GMT it is 7 am in New York (**a**).

put forward one hour in spring and back one hour in autumn. The maps below do not reflect DST adjustments.

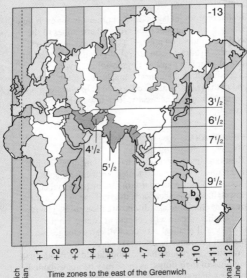

Time zones to the east of the Greenwich Meridian are 'later' than GMT. For example, at 12 noon GMT it is 10 pm in Sydney (**b**).

- easily fatigued
- less efficient than usual
- liable to suffer memory lapses
- physically under par

Recovery from jet lag takes about one day for each time zone (15° of longitude) you cross. (Time zones of the world are shown on pp.46–7.) If you have important business to attend to on arrival, if possible advance the date of your trip to allow time to adjust. Avoid excessive alcohol and heavy meals during the flight, and perhaps take a mild sedative to help you sleep on the aircraft and, if necessary, for a few nights after arrival.

SEA TRAVEL
Medical facilities on board

Most large passenger liners have full medical facilities and trained medical staff to deal with emergencies, illness and injury on board. In rare instances when hospitalization is necessary, the staff can arrange for treatment on shore at a disembarkation point. The type and quality of care will depend, of course, on the country. All medical services will carry charges, so medical insurance is crucial (see p.25–7).

Travellers on regular medication should carry adequate supplies of their drugs, as these may be unavailable in places where the ship has planned stops. Most medications for common minor complaints – including sea sickness – will be available on board.

If you have special needs or a pre-existing medical condition that might require attention, consult with the

shipping company in advance to confirm that the
necessary equipment and staff will be on board.

Hazards

Sea voyages present a few unique hazards to travellers.
Fortunately, they are relatively easy to prevent.

- Stairways, gangways and decks can be slippery when
  wet (from rain or having been washed down by the
  crew), so always wear sensible, slip-resistant shoes
  when moving about the ship. Also, be aware that
  some medications – including some sea sickness
  remedies – can affect your balance and judgement
  and make falls more likely.
- The sun's rays can be stronger and more damaging at
  sea; always use a high-factor sunscreen on all areas
  of exposed skin and wear sunglasses.

Keeping fit at sea

Sea travel is restful and invigorating, and a cruise is an
ideal way of recuperating after periods of illness or
stress.

Particularly on long sea voyages, it's important to try
and remain physically active. Luckily this isn't difficult
– most cruise ships have a tempting programme of
sport and leisure activities.

Follow the same rules as you would for exercise at
home:

- Short periods of regular exercise are better for you
  and safer than one strenuous burst.
- Warm up properly before anything demanding such
  as tennis, aerobics or jogging.
- Build up gradually. Don't spoil a longed-for holiday
  by injuring yourself with activity you're not used to.

ROAD TRAVEL
Preparation

Long-distance road travel is tiring, especially if you are driving. In a foreign country this may mean driving on the right-hand side of the road, following different driving regulations, and reading foreign road signs. Plan to minimize the strain. If possible:

- Share the driving with someone else.
- In countries where driving is on the right-hand side of the road, hire a car rather than taking your right-hand drive car.
- Check car accessories suppliers for headrests, backrests and other devices that will maximize your comfort and safety. Take these with you.
- Pack a few tapes to relax and entertain you, especially if you have children in the car.
- Check that your car is in perfect order, conforms to regulations in the country in which you will be driving, and that lights are adapted for that country.
- Join an international motoring organization (such as the AA) and arrange insurance cover for you and your passengers against breakdown, accident, fire and illness.
- Study the highway codes (available from motoring organizations and national tourist offices) for the country to which you are travelling.
- Hire a carphone for emergency use in remote areas.
- Plan your route to take in frequent stops and, if you can, bypass cities (see pp.11–12 for more advice).
- If hiring a car and travelling with an infant, check that your car hire firm provides car seats. If it does not, bring your own.

- Take a medical kit (see pp.30–1). Motorists are required to carry one in many countries.
- Obtain easy-to-read road maps of the areas to which you will be travelling.

Driving time

The adaptation to driving in a foreign country causes mental strain, and this causes tiredness and dangerous lapses of concentration. Plan your route to minimize strain and tiredness. Long-distance truck drivers are subjected to rigorous health regulations governing driving and resting time. These regulations are geared to vehicle weight, but if you are the only car driver, and/or if you are towing a trailer, it is sensible to observe them. They include the following:

- Do not drive for more than nine hours in one day, or 90 hours total in two weeks.
- Do not drive for more than 4½ hours without a stop of 45 minutes, or three stops of at least 15 minutes.
- Have a rest period of 9 to 11 hours in every 24-hour period.
- Break for 24 to 36 consecutive hours every week.

Night driving

Start early to avoid driving through the night. You may find the traffic quieter at night, but sleepiness may make night driving very risky, and the lights of oncoming traffic can be exhausting.

In some developing countries it can be extremely dangerous to drive at night as roads may be poorly maintained. There may be no road markings; you may encounter hazards such as vehicles parked without lights on road sides; and large wild animals stray on to the roads at night. In sparsely populated areas you may be unable to get any help if you break down or have an accident.

WHEN NOT TO DRIVE

You should continually assess your own fitness to drive when travelling. Do not drive if:

- you feel tired or unwell. Fatigue causes serious accidents.
- you have to take medicines (see below). They can seriously affect your ability to drive.
- you have been drinking. Driving in unfamiliar conditions may affect your ability to respond quickly, and alcohol will make this worse. Furthermore, remember that in many countries drink-drive laws are even stricter then in the UK (see p.34).

Medicines

If you need medicines while you are travelling, read the instructions carefully, and ask your doctor or pharmacist if you should drive when taking them. Not all medicines affect driving skills.

Those that *do not affect driving* include:

- over-the-counter painkillers such as aspirin and Nurofen
- antibiotics – but check the label carefully
- antacids
- anti-diarrhoea medication
- anti-fungal drugs
- non-narcotic cough mixtures
- throat lozenges

Any drugs which slow down your speed of reaction or ability to assess driving situations must not be used while you're driving.

Those that *do affect driving* include:

- antihistamines
- sedatives, including cold cures, e.g. Night Nurse
- narcotic painkillers
- antidepressants
- amphetamine-like weight control medication
- travel sickness medication (Fortunately, travel sickness rarely affects the driver.)

Fatigue

Driving demands great concentration, and this is exhausting if it is not relieved. In long-distance driving it can make you fall asleep at the wheel. Concentration, especially when following an unfamiliar route, can also cause tension, leading to headaches and stiffness. Sharing the driving is one way to minimize the strain. Other methods are described in the box below.

RELIEVING FATIGUE AND STIFFNESS

- Adjust the seat before starting out; use a backrest and cushions if necessary.
- Stop driving if you feel tired.
- Break frequently for rests.
- Break for meals and snacks, but avoid large, heavy meals and alcohol.
- Make sure the car is well ventilated. Don't let it become too hot.
- Move your shoulders and neck regularly while driving.
- If time allows, stop once every hour to walk about.
- Take more active exercises, such as handball, rowing or tennis, on days when you are not travelling.

TRAVELLING WHILE PREGNANT

Sitting in a confined space for long periods impairs blood circulation. In pregnancy this increases the risk of thrombosis (blood clots) in the veins of the legs. When travelling by air or road, stand up and walk once an hour. While sitting, do the simple exercises listed on p.88. Whatever method of travel you choose, try to make room for an improvised footrest that will take pressure off the backs of the thighs.

If you travel by car, fit a seat belt for pregnant women which does not pass across the abdomen. You also may be more comfortable with a backrest while in the car.

3. Staying healthy

PREVENTING DISEASE

Many of the world's most serious infectious diseases
are the result of economic deprivation and poor living
standards. In general, the local population is more at
risk than the visitor; travellers can more easily limit
their exposure to the causes of most diseases.

Disease organisms

Most diseases are transmitted by one of the following
types of organism:

- bacteria: carriers of infections such as diphtheria and
  tuberculosis
- viruses: microscopic parasites carrying diseases such
  as the common cold and flu
- rickettsiae: germs that are commonly found in insects
  and cause various diseases, including typhus
- fungi: non-green plants that cause ringworm,
  athlete's foot, thrush, etc.
- protozoa: parasites that cause diseases such as
  malaria
- metazoa: many-celled parasites including
  roundworms, flukes, tapeworms, lice and fleas

Spreading disease

The following are some of the ways disease is
commonly spread.

- Many germs are spread by direct human contact,
  such as kissing, sexual intercourse and holding
  hands.

- Droplets of moisture are frequent carriers of bacteria and viruses; the droplets may be coughed, spat, sneezed or breathed out, and then inhaled by other people.
- Dust may harbour infected airborne particles which are later inhaled by others.
- Objects such as washcloths, handkerchiefs and towels that have been used by infected persons are ideal breeding grounds for bacteria.
- Pets and farm animals may be carriers of diseases or parasites.
- Insects, especially flies, are frequently carriers of disease, and are particularly drawn to uncovered food, which they then contaminate.
- Dirt entering a break in the skin often harbours disease.
- Contaminated food or water, or dirty utensils, can harbour and transmit germs.
- Parasitic animals such as mosquitoes, ticks and fleas can transmit disease to the host.

General guidelines on avoiding diseases are given in the box opposite, and guidelines for children, pregnant travellers and those with special needs are given in the box overleaf.

This chapter describes several of the most common hazards to health encountered by travellers. See Chapter 6 for more information on specific diseases (where they occur, symptoms, and how to avoid them). Immunization is available for many of them.

STEPS TO AVOID DISEASE WHILE ABROAD

Eating and drinking

- Never drink water that you are unsure of. If in doubt, drink bottled water.
- Avoid ice in drinks. It is often made from local water and may contain disease organisms.
- Wash all fruit and vegetables in bottled or sterilized water before eating.
- Do not eat food that you have reason to believe has not been hygienically prepared. Avoid dirty restaurants.
- Never eat uncooked food, especially pork, fish or shellfish, or food that has been kept warm.
- Never eat food that is exposed to flies.
- Don't eat locally made ice cream in high-risk areas; the salmonella typhoid organism can survive freezing.

See pp.94–101 for more on food and water health hazards.

Personal hygiene

- Always wash your hands after visiting the toilet.
- Always wash your hands before touching, preparing or eating food.
- Keep your hands away from your eyes and mouth unless you have washed them. Viruses can enter the body by these routes also.
- Avoid washing or bathing in polluted water or water which may harbour disease organisms.

Activities

- Avoid unprotected sexual intercourse.

Medical

- Ensure that you have the correct inoculations before travelling.
- Treat all insect bites immediately and seriously.

General

- Use insect repellents, mosquito nets, etc. where necessary.

DISEASE PREVENTION FOR CHILDREN

Sensible precautions can minimize the health risks of travelling with babies and children. Careful attention to hygiene is the best preventive measure in poor and tropical countries. Explain to older children why they must:

- wash their hands thoroughly before eating and after going to the lavatory, and never put their fingers in their mouths
- always wear shoes
- never sit on the ground or play in soil or dirt
- swim only in regularly chlorinated swimming pools
- drink only boiled or bottled water (see pp.99–100 for more on drinking water safety)
- avoid playing with stray cats or dogs, or any other wild animals who may carry disease.

DISEASE PREVENTION FOR PREGNANT TRAVELLERS

Pay attention to hygiene to avoid colds, flu, infections, worms, and diarrhoea. Swim only in swimming pools that are regularly cleaned and properly disinfected.

Some diseases are a danger only to pregnant women and their fetuses:

Toxoplasmosis This is an infection by a microscopic organism which can affect the fetal nervous system. It is often transmitted by eating undercooked meat and by handling kittens, which are infected after weaning.

Listeriosis This is a harmful bacterial infection present in poultry and untreated milk. Do not drink or eat unpasteurized milk or milk products, such as cheese, or eat undercooked or reheated poultry.

Others are dangerous for anyone but particularly to a pregnant woman and her fetus:

Malaria If you are going to a malaria region, protect yourself by covering your skin at dawn and dusk, sleeping under a mosquito net and taking antimalarial tablets.

Some antimalarial drugs can harm an embryo or early fetus. Chloroquine and Paludrine are safe in pregnancy; Mefloquine may affect the developing baby during the first three months; pyrimethamine, Maloprim, primaquine and sulphadoxine may be hazardous.

Spray your bedroom with insect repellents before going to bed, but do not overdo it, and try to avoid inhaling the vapour. Some repellents may harm the fetus.

DISEASE PREVENTION FOR TRAVELLERS WITH SPECIAL MEDICAL CONDITIONS

Even minor illnesses can be devastating to travellers with special medical conditions. If you have a medical condition that might make you particularly vulnerable, you should know what precautions to take and what warning signs to look out for.

Diabetic travellers

Any illness, however minor, that disrupts regular food intake can be serious for diabetics. These include traveller's diarrhoea and travel sickness. You might need to take preventive antibiotics. In insulin-dependent travellers, illnesses that affect food intake can lead to hypoglycaemia. Diabetics who are not insulin-dependent may need to take insulin temporarily during an illness or infection.

Travellers on regular medication

If you take regular medications, you should consult your doctor to determine whether any of these conflict with medications commonly prescribed for minor travel illnesses or with any preventive drug treatment, such as antimalarial drugs.

HIV-positive travellers

Travellers with impaired immune function may develop what are known as 'opportunistic infections' – including internal fungal infections and *pneumocystis carinii* pneumonia (PCP). They may also be more at risk of very severe symptoms of what in others might be relatively minor illnesses. For this reason, HIV-positive travellers in particular should be sure to take every precaution against disease as outlined in this chapter. Seek advice from your doctor about other measures.

DIARRHOEA

Travellers' diarrhoea

This is the most common infection suffered by travellers. It usually has nothing to do with the stress of travel, a change of food or water or the local wine. At least 75 per cent of all cases of travellers' diarrhoea are caused by bacteria, in particular faecal organisms. The most common route of transmission is the faecal–oral route: eating food that has been handled by someone who has not washed his or her hands after using the toilet. Because bacteria can only be seen with a microscope, such contamination is seldom visible. Direct person-to-person spread of bacteria is also possible. Swimming pools are occasionally responsible for spread of a few types of faecal organisms that can resist chlorination for a time. Many beaches and the adjacent waters are now contaminated by sewage outflows. The survival of such organisms is also encouraged by higher temperatures.

TREATING DIARRHOEA

Most mild travellers' diarrhoea will disappear in two or three days. In such cases, the only treatment that is usually required is rehydration if there has been a significant loss of fluid. For adults, this involves increasing regular (non-alcoholic) fluid intake.

Controlling the diarrhoea with antidiarrhoeal agents (e.g. Imodium, Arret) is only recommended for short periods when access to toilet facilities is limited (e.g. a long bus or car journey). These drugs should never be given to children, and they should never be used for long periods because they can prolong the infection and prohibit the body from flushing it out.

You can get up-to-date information on the state of British beaches from the *Heinz Good Beach Guide*. Most travellers experience mild diarrhoea in spite of taking precautions. Nevertheless, minimize the risk by:

- avoiding suspect food and water
- washing your hands after using the toilet and every time you handle food.

Advice for preventing food poisoning appears on p.95. There are three circumstances in which you need medical attention for diarrhoea. These are for diarrhoea:

- that lasts for longer than seven days (three days in children, one day in babies)

DEHYDRATION

Dehydration is especially dangerous for babies (who can become critically ill very quickly), the elderly and pregnant women (it can affect the fetus). It can result from watery diarrhoea, in which much liquid is lost, and also from prolonged exposure to heat and not enough fluid intake. Watch for the warning signs.

Signs of dehydration

- dry mouth
- no urination
- dry skin
- smelly urine
- weakness

For anyone who is particularly vulnerable, electrolyte rehydration solutions (e.g. Dioralyte) are essential to replenish fluids and other lost constituents (e.g. sodium and potassium) without delay. Plain water is not enough. Carry rehydrating solution or powder with you.

If you do not have rehydration solution, you can make your own by adding a pinch of salt and one teaspoon of sugar or honey to 250 ml (1 large cup) of clean water.

Rehydration can be life-saving, so don't wait until a doctor arrives if you suspect dehydration.

- with blood or bloody mucus in the stools
- associated with fever, illness or other general upset

In such cases you may need a stool test to discover the specific cause and, if appropriate, be prescribed antibiotic treatment. You should also drink plenty of fluids and avoid solid food until the diarrhoea disappears.

DIARRHOEA AND CONTRACEPTION

Bear in mind that an attack of diarrhoea can flush any medication you are on out of your system. So if you are on the Pill, use condoms to minimize the risk of unwanted pregnancy.

DYSENTERY

Blood or mucus in the stools is a sign of dysentery. The main symptom is diarrhoea, but because dysentery can lead to serious complications, it is important to be able to distinguish dysentery from diarrhoea. If blood or bloody mucus appears in the stools, you should seek medical advice and have a laboratory analysis of your stools to determine the cause.

There are two types of dysentery: bacillary dysentery (shigellosis) and amoebic dysentery (amoebiasis) (see table opposite). They are treated with different antibiotics. Amoebiasis is the more severe and long lasting – symptoms can disappear and recur for months. In addition to antibiotic treatment, rehydration is essential, especially for babies, pregnant women and the elderly (see box on p.61).

TYPES OF DYSENTERY AND THEIR EFFECT

Bacillary dysentery causes:

- inflammation and ulceration of the large intestine (colon) and the lower part of the small intestine
- high fever and nausea or vomiting
- diarrhoea of increasing frequency, commonly up to 20 or more bowel actions a day
- stools characteristically streaked with mucus and blood

The severity varies greatly, but it usually disappears in a week with treatment.

Amoebic dysentery causes:

- mild and vague symptoms that may not become noticeable until well after you have returned from your trip abroad
- low-grade stomach discomfort
- a general feeling of being unwell (malaise)
- mild diarrhoea with blood and mucus
- sometimes tenderness over the liver (upper right side of the abdomen)

Amoebic dysentery may lead to liver abscesses. Symptoms are:

- fever and weakness
- nausea
- pain in the right shoulder
- loss of appetite
- yellowness of the skin and eyes (jaundice)
- loss of weight

If you experience the above symptoms, get medical attention.

FEVER

A fever is a rise in body temperature above the normal temperature of 37° C (98.6° F). Causes include:

- bacterial or viral infection
- excessive loss of body fluid
- excessive heat to the head
- heart attack

- overactive thyroid gland
- lymphoma tumour

In addition to the temperature rise there may be other associated symptoms. These include:

- sweating
- shivering
- headaches
- flushed skin
- thirst
- confusion

Many fevers are temporary and not serious, including those associated with common viruses such as flu. In these cases, symptoms can be relieved with aspirin or, for children, paracetamol. (Never give aspirin to a fevered child under 12 years of age; it may promote Reye's syndrome, a serious liver and brain disorder.)

In addition to giving aspirin or paracetamol, fevers can be reduced by:

- removing clothes
- sponging down repeatedly with cool-to-tepid water
- if possible, bathing in cool-to-tepid water

Seek medical attention immediately if:

- the fever persists for more than a few days
- the fever is very high. High fevers can result in brain damage, and are especially dangerous for children
- you are in a malarial area. Fever is one of the most common symptoms of the disease
- fever is accompanied by other symptoms, including vomiting, diarrhoea, severe headache, neck stiffness, rashes or evidence of insect bites or stings

COLDS AND FLU

Travellers are susceptible to colds and flu in foreign countries, since they do not have natural immunities to many of the native bugs. Take with you the remedies that work best for you. If you are flying, take a decongestant spray to use during the flight, when cabin pressurization could cause discomfort (see pp.41–3). If you get a cold, rest if you feel ill and take your usual medication. See a doctor if you get bronchitis or any other chest ailment.

SKIN COMPLAINTS

Cuts and grazes

In tropical areas, particularly, it is important to clean minor cuts and grazes thoroughly and to keep them clean. A small cut can quickly turn septic. Take antiseptic lotion or cream in your medical kit (see pp.30–1). If you do not have your kit with you, wash the cut with soap and water you know to be clean, and cover it, then clean and disinfect it as soon as you can.

Rashes

There is little you can do to treat a rash, but if it itches, cool it by bathing it with cold water and dust it with talcum powder. Cool showers are the remedy for prickly heat, a rash caused by excessive sweating (see pp.106–7).

You should note the progress of a rash and see a doctor if it persists or spreads. Rashes are often a reaction to some minor allergy and die down quickly, but they can also be a feature of some serious diseases.

HAY FEVER AND ASTHMA

Hay fever

This disorder, with symptoms similar to those of a bad head cold, is caused by an allergic reaction to pollens, mainly from trees, but also from flowers and grasses. It affects millions of people during springtime and early summer. The symptoms, including sneezing, stinging and watering eyes, a runny nose and tiredness, are irritating on a holiday and they prevent you from driving and enjoying sports.

● Antihistamines are effective, but may cause drowsiness.

Asthma

This is a potentially life-threatening disorder in which the bronchial tubes in the lungs contract in spasm, causing wheezing or, in acute attacks, seriously interfering with breathing. It may also be caused by an allergy, and often accompanies hay fever. Air pollution in cities is now known to cause asthma attacks.

Pollen seasons

If you get hay fever or are prone to asthma you would be wise to try and travel outside the season when plants are shedding pollen. This process, which takes place in late spring/early summer in temperate regions (such as northern Europe), happens at other times of year in different climatic zones. The authorities in many regions, including many states in the US, publish pollen maps. Use them to decide when not to take a holiday in the tropics or the Mediterranean – and, indeed, where to go to escape from high pollen counts at home. (See also Helplines, pp.245–7.)

BITES AND STINGS

Always take these seriously, mainly because of the major risk of infection. Children can be very seriously affected by bites and stings from scorpions and poisonous spiders. Explain the dangers to them, showing them pictures of poisonous species and where they may be found. (For instance, scorpions are known to hide in shoes; see p.82.) Spray children's clothes

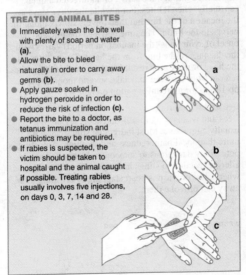

TREATING ANIMAL BITES

- Immediately wash the bite well with plenty of soap and water (a).
- Allow the bite to bleed naturally in order to carry away germs (b).
- Apply gauze soaked in hydrogen peroxide in order to reduce the risk of infection (c).
- Report the bite to a doctor, as tetanus immunization and antibiotics may be required.
- If rabies is suspected, the victim should be taken to hospital and the animal caught if possible. Treating rabies usually involves five injections, on days 0, 3, 7, 14 and 28.

with permethrin to repel mosquitoes and ticks, but do not apply insect repellents containing a high concentration of DEET to the skin or near the eyes (see box on pp.76–7 describing insect repellents).

Rabies Almost any animal can transmit rabies, and domestic dogs and cats readily acquire the infection if exposed to infected wild animals. The virus is transmitted through the saliva of an infected animal, especially when it bites. For a while the virus stays at the location of the bite but then travels slowly along the nerves to the brain. The time between the bite and the onset of symptoms (the incubation period) varies with the distance of the bite from the brain. Severe bites on the head or neck may result in rabies in nine days; bites remote from the head may take several months. (See pp.183–6 for more information on rabies.)

Bee and wasp stings

Bees and wasps sting in self-defence; they are not usually aggressive. Most individual stings cause no more than local pain, redness and swelling. Any sting is potentially dangerous to someone who has had an allergic reaction to stings in the past. Try to be calm when a bee or wasp is near: slapping or brushing them away can provoke them.

wasp   bee

TREATING STINGS

After stinging, bees, wasps and hornets usually fly off, leaving the stinger protruding from your skin.

- Never use tweezers to remove the stinger. If you do, you will inject more venom by squeezing the venom sac.
- Use the edge of a credit card, fingernail or nailfile to scrape away from the direction in which the stinger entered the skin (**a**).
- Remember that the bite opening can allow germs to get in, so wash the area well, but gently, with soap and water (**b**).
- Apply an icecube in a handkerchief (**c**). This closes blood vessels and decreases absorption of venom.
- Apply a soothing lotion.
- If symptoms are severe take an antihistamine tablet by mouth.

If there have been hundreds of stings, seek medical attention and watch for signs of allergic reaction (anaphylaxis).

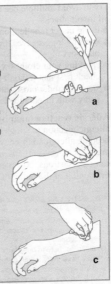

Multiple stings These can be dangerous. A large dose of insect toxin can cause:

- much local swelling
- burning and itching lasting days
- in severe cases, even unconsciousness
- drowsiness
- fever
- headache
- muscle pains
- cramps

Try to avoid multiple bee and wasp stings as you would all insect attacks:

- using insect repellent on all areas of exposed skin
- wearing long sleeves, trousers and socks when outdoors
- spraying your clothes with insect repellent (But check first that it won't ruin your clothes.)
- sleeping under mosquito nets, which you can also spray with insect repellent

Allergic reaction (anaphylaxis) Fortunately, an allergic reaction to stings is rare. If someone has become allergic to insect venom as a result of a previous sting – perhaps years before – a further sting can be disastrous, however. The main danger is ballooning of the lining of the voice box (laryngeal

---

TREATING ANAPHYLAXIS

- Rush the affected person to hospital where he or she can receive adrenaline, intravenous antihistamine and steroids, and – if necessary – tracheostomy and cardiopulmonary resuscitation.
- While en route to hospital, the priority is air for the victim. You may have to try mouth-to-mouth ventilation.
- If the symptoms are associated with a sting on an arm or a leg and there is a known history of severe reaction to insect stings, consider using a tourniquet just above the sting if there is likely to be a delay in getting to hospital. *But this must never be so tight as to eliminate an arterial pulse below it.* Such a tourniquet could be life saving but *must* be loosened briefly every five minutes to maintain blood flow.
- If the victim is conscious and can swallow normally, give an aspirin tablet. This is not to relieve pain but to combat the toxin causing the reaction.

oedema) and near closure of the air tubes of the lungs (bronchospasm). These effects can be so severe as to cut off the air supply completely, suffocating the victim. Emergency help is vital. Indications that anaphylaxis is occurring are:

- wheezing and coughing
- obvious difficulty in breathing
- swelling of parts of the body away from the bite, especially in the face
- severe itching
- raised, purplish areas on other parts of skin

Insect bites

For the most part, insect bites are an annoyance but not a serious health hazard. The discomfort and itchiness they cause usually disappear within a few days. The results of multiple mosquito, midge or sandfly bites can be extreme, however, and may spoil your pleasure in being outdoors. More seriously, and especially in the tropics, insects like mosquitoes and fleas can transmit dangerous diseases like malaria (see table on pp.74–5). For more information on these specific diseases, see Chapter 6. An essential part of preventing these diseases and reducing the amount of irritation caused by harmless insects is to avoid being bitten: for details on insect repellents, see the box on pp.76–7.

Bedbugs These are broad, reddish, flat, blood-sucking insects that feed on mammals. They are found in temperate regions all over the world where people live.

- If you suspect bedbugs exists where you are sleeping, move the bed to the centre of the room and sleep with the light on.

Black flies cause painful bites and can so swell the eyelids as to close an eye for weeks. They appear in several parts of the world, including parts of Asia, Africa and the Americas. In tropical Africa and regions of South and Central America, they transmit the form of filariasis known as river blindness (onchocerciasis).

Chiggers, or harvest mites, are commonly encountered in the fields in autumn all over the world. They often remain feeding on the skin for several days, too tiny to see. Chiggers transmit a form of typhus, known as scrub typhus, especially in Southeast Asia.

Fleas are small, wingless, blood-sucking insects, which have enormously well-developed muscular hind legs that are adapted for jumping. They exist all over the world. Most fleas are no more than a nuisance, but the oriental rat flea is the transmitter of bubonic plague from rats to humans. Fleas live in the bedding of livestock and pets and in carpets and rugs, as well as on animals themselves. An adult flea may live for a year. Some kinds of flea remain attached to their hosts for long periods.

- Tuck your bedding into the mattress to discourage fleas from jumping into your bed from the floor.
- Place the legs of your bed into pots of water; this keeps fleas from climbing from the floor into your bed.

Mosquitoes suck blood from a human host, causing itchy bites. They exist worldwide, and in some regions they transmit malaria, yellow fever, filariasis, and dengue through infected saliva. They are not considered to spread AIDS.

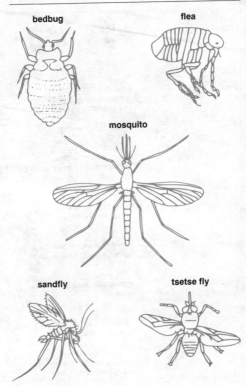

bedbug

flea

mosquito

sandfly

tsetse fly

INSECT BITES

INSECT	CHARACTERISTICS OF BITES
Anopheles mosquito	persistently irritating bites
Bedbug	irritation, inflammation, can cause allergic reaction and secondary infection
Black fly	severe bites, swelling
Chiggers (mites)	intense itching, scabies-like irritation (tiny, scaly swellings)
Flea	varies from no reaction to pain and swelling
Midge	pricking sensation, skin bumps, fever in extreme cases
Sand fly	itching, pain, lasting spots
Tick	varies from no reaction to pain, ulceration
Tsetse fly	pain, frequently swelling from allergic reaction

TIME & PLACE	DISEASES
night indoors outdoors	malaria filariasis yellow fever dengue
night indoors	hepatitis B
daytime outdoors	onchocerciosis (river blindness)
night daytime indoors outdoors	typhus scabies
night daytime indoors	plague
evening outdoors in swarms	filariasis
evening indoors outdoors	leishmaniasis
night daytime outdoors	lyme disease encephalitis
daytime indoors	sleeping sickness

Sandflies cause irritating bites which may leave a spot that is troublesome for weeks. They are found in parts of Africa, Asia and the Americas. In some regions they transmit sandfly fever, Leishmaniasis and Oroya fever. **Ticks** are very small, blood-sucking insects that are often inconspicuous once they have attached to a human or animal host. They continue to suck blood and swell until they are removed. They appear worldwide in temperate regions, and they spread Lyme disease, which occurs in the USA and Europe, and encephalitis,

---

INSECT REPELLENTS

In addition to covering as much exposed skin as possible when outdoors (especially at dusk), using effective insect repellents is an essential measure in preventing insect (in particular mosquito) bites, especially when travelling in a malarial area.

Repellents come in several forms: sprays (both pump and aerosol), gels, lotions, and roll-on sticks. In addition, a number of substances form the basis for repellents:

● Among the most effective ones are those with **DEET** (diethyltoluamide). These can be messy, have an unpleasant odour and may be toxic, especially when used in high concentrations. Repellents with a DEET concentration of 50–80 percent are usually recommended (at the lower end of this scale for children and pregnant women). Also avoid contact with cameras; DEET can damage plastics. These repellents are not recommended for use over extended periods (i.e. months). As with all repellents, avoid contact with eyes and mouth. These repellents are effective for a few hours on the skin, and they must be reapplied after swimming. Before bed, wash your skin thoroughly to remove all repellent. Watch for any itching, rashes or blisters that may result from use, and if they occur, see a doctor immediately. DEET can be safely applied to clothes, and is especially useful on socks, as many biting insects attack the ankles.

which occurs in Europe.

- To remove ticks, apply nail polish to the tick and surrounding site; this causes the tick to detach itself and allows you to remove it entirely. Be very careful if trying to remove it with tweezers; you might remove the body but leave the head in place, and the tick will grow again.

Tsetse flies are found in Africa, where they transmit sleeping sickness (African trypanosomiasis).

- A safe but powerful natural repellent is now available from MASTA (see Helplines, pp.245–7). Mosi-guard is made from **Eucalyptus oils** and comes in spray, stick and gel forms. All last up to seven hours.
- **Citronella** is a plant with repelling properties; it is often applied as an oil directly to the skin. It is not as powerful as DEET-based repellents, but it has a more pleasant, lemon smell.
- Clothes, furniture and bed nets can be sprayed with an insecticide containing **pyrethrin** (or **permethrin**, the synthetic form). (You can purchase nets impregnated with permethrin.) So-called 'knockdown' sprays containing permethrin will kill mosquitoes and other insects inside your room or bed net. These are considered safe for adults, children and pets.

Other repelling products available include:
- **Mosquito coils.** These are often used at night (both indoors and on porches and verandahs) and have the advantage of being usable anywhere; you simply light them and they give off permethrin smoke for several hours.
- **Vaporizing mats.** These work like coils, releasing permethrin over a period of hours, and are also used at night indoors. They require electricity, however.
- **Buzzers**, whose signal is alleged to deter female (biting) mosquitoes, have not been proved to be effective.

Snake bites

Venomous snakes occur worldwide except in the
Antarctic, at altitudes above about 5000 m, and on
some islands, including most Caribbean islands, Crete,
Iceland, Ireland, Madagascar, New Zealand, and most
Pacific islands. Even in regions where they exist,

1 Cobra
2 Krait
3 Viper

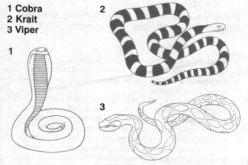

however, they are most likely to be found in rural areas
and are more of a risk to local populations than to
travellers, who are usually better protected. If travelling
off the beaten track, however, or engaging in outdoor
activities in a snake-infested area, the risk of
encountering a venomous snake is increased.

About half of all snake bites are harmless. Even when
bitten, only about 10 per cent of snake-bite victims die.
Venomous snakes include vipers, cobras, kraits,
mambas, tiger snakes, coral snakes, rattlesnakes,
moccasins, asps and adders. All have fangs at the front

PREVENTING SNAKE BITES

● Do not disturb or handle snakes.
● If a snake appears ready to strike, keep still until it has moved on.
● Avoid swimming in fresh water (lakes and rivers) in the tropics – they might harbour venomous snakes.
● Watch where you walk; stepping on a snake can provoke it.
● If camping in an area with venomous snakes, raise your bed off the ground.

of their mouths, and their bites can be distinguished from those of non-poisonous snakes by the fang puncture marks above the bite. Their venom affects the nervous system, causing:

● vomiting
● drooping of the eyelids
● difficulty in swallowing
● paralysis of breathing
● low blood pressure
● muscle weakness
● coughing

There is seldom any immediate swelling at the site of the bite, but swelling may develop later in the case of cobra bites.

Sea snakes occur in coastal waters of Asia and the Pacific. Their venom affects muscles, causing similar effects but also severe muscle pain and more marked paralysis.

Vipers, which include adders, rattlesnakes and Asian pit vipers, produce a venom that attacks the blood. The effects are:

● marked immediate swelling at the site of the bite
● vomiting
● low blood pressure

- severe internal bleeding
- continued swelling for two to three days
- spontaneous bruising of the skin
- blisters forming around the bite
- tissue destruction, with a putrid smell, at the site of the bite

Local doctors know about snake bite and have access to antivenoms. See one immediately.

TREATING SNAKE BITES
- The victim must be made to rest in order to slow the heart down, thereby reducing poison absorption. If an arm or leg is bitten, keep it flat.
- Clean the wound by wiping away from the bite (**a**). Remove any venom that may be around the wound. Do not cut into the bite or attempt to suck out the venom.
- Reduce the spread of venom by applying firm pressure bandaging to the area of the bite (**b**).
- Get the victim to a hospital or to a doctor as quickly as possible.

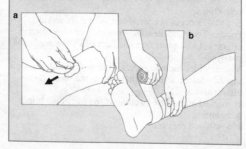

Spider bites

The great majority of spiders are harmless. Those few that are potentially dangerous will mostly avoid humans, but may be encountered in shady corners of outside toilets, sheds and house basements. The most dangerous are the black widow and brown recluse spiders (North America), tarantula (Mediterrannean), banana spider (South America), and the funnel web and red-back spiders (Australia). They are most dangerous to young children.

Bites from these spiders cause:

- burning pain at the site of the bite
- fever
- low blood pressure
- collapse
- pain in the muscles
- nausea and vomiting
- sweating
- fast, weak pulse

**Black
widow
spider**

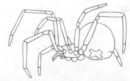

TREATING SPIDER BITES
- Any victim of a suspected venomous spider bite should get medical help immediately.
- Apply ice and immobilize the area.
- Medical staff will treat spider bites with a slow intravenous injection of 10 per cent calcium gluconate and, if necessary, the specific antivenom.
- Where tissue damage has occurred, surgery may be necessary.

Scorpion stings

Scorpions are common in the tropics and subtropics, and a sting can be lethal. Between 1000 and 2000 people die every year from scorpion stings in Mexico, for example. Children are particularly vulnerable. The scorpion's poison glands are in the tip segment of the tail, and these open into a single pointed sting that produces a single puncture.

scorpion

The immediate signs of scorpion bites are:
● severe pain at the site of the sting
● local swelling, redness and bruising
● nausea and vomiting
● salivation
● sweating
● breathing difficulty
● wide pupils

TREATING SCORPION BITES
● Apply firm pressure bandaging at the site to help minimize absorption of the venom.
● Give painkillers if necessary.
● Medical staff can give a specific antivenom.
● Find a doctor at once.

Centipede and millipede bites

Centipedes and millipedes are found in many parts of the world. Although quite common, they are not a high risk for travellers.

Centipedes can inflict painful bites with swelling and inflammation, but in most cases the effects are local and there is no danger to life. If centipede venom gets into the circulation it may cause:

- headache
- vomiting
- irregularity of the heart
- convulsions

Millipedes can squirt a powerful venom containing hydrogen cyanide and other dangerous substances. This is especially harmful to the eyes and can even cause blindness, if neglected. The venom causes staining, blistering and peeling of the skin. There is little risk from these large insects unless they are picked up.

centipede

millipede

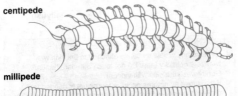

TREATING CENTIPEDE AND MILLIPEDE BITES

Venom should be washed off with a copious and prolonged flow of water. Eye washing is particularly important. There is no antivenom for either centipede or millipede bites.

Marine creatures

Jellyfish carry stinging capsules called nematocysts which discharge an irritating substance into the skin when touched. Usually, this causes no more than an itchy rash, which may persist for a day or two. Some species, notably the box jellyfish of the Pacific and Indian oceans, can cause more serious symptoms including:

- local pain
- vomiting
- diarrhoea
- paralysis
  of the
  muscles
  of respiration
- a drop in blood
  pressure

jellyfish

TREATING JELLYFISH STINGS

- Remove any visible tentacles attached to the skin with tweezers or sticky tape. Do not touch with bare hands.
- Gently wash the skin with vinegar.
- If the above symptoms occur, a tourniquet is needed to prevent the venom from being absorbed. This is best done by a doctor, so find medical attention urgently.

Venomous fish, such as stingrays and scorpionfish, usually inhabit warm tropical coastal waters, especially tropical coral reefs. They can occur in temperate regions, however, such as along the coast of Cornwall.

Stingrays will sting only if you step on one, so you
should, if possible, always watch where you tread while
in water. Shuffling slowly and prodding in front of you
with a stick while you walk will also help.

Scorpionfish, which include the stonefishes and zebra
fishes, on the other hand, will sting aggressively using
their spines. The symptoms, in either case, are:

- severe pain at the
  sting site
- nausea and vomiting
- severe tissue damage
  at the sting site
- local swelling
- diarrhoea
- heart irregularity

Stonefish

Stingray

FOOT PROBLEMS

Try to have at least two pairs of sturdy shoes or boots
appropriate for the climate so that you can change
footwear if one pair becomes damp or your feet begin
to ache. If you are using new shoes, be sure to break
them in well before you go; most new shoes, no matter
how well they fit, will cause blisters at first.

If your feet develop any of the problems listed here,
deal with them immediately and allow time for rests
when you can take the pressure off your feet.

Corns and calluses

Rubbing against the foot may cause a hard patch of
shiny yellow skin known as a callus. A corn is a
condition which often develops from a callus. Do not
try to cut these off. Instead, soak your feet in warm
water and massage the area. Minimize the pain and
pressure by padding the area around the corn or callus
using soft 'animal' wool (available from a pharmacy)
or similar. Take a packet of corn plasters with you.

Bunions

A bunion may develop as a joint becomes swollen and
deformed, usually as a result of pointed shoes. Effective
long-term treatment requires surgery, but you may be
able to relieve the discomfort by changing your
footwear. Avoid shoes that are pointed or too narrow.

Achilles tendonitis

This is an inflammation of the Achilles tendon
(connecting the calf muscles to the heel of the foot). It
is usually caused by poor footwear that places strain on
the heel. Change your shoes if this occurs.

Blisters

Friction between the skin and ill-fitting footwear may cause a fluid-filled blister. Small blisters can be covered with a plaster and will probably disappear; larger ones should be pricked with a sterile needle and then pressed with an antiseptic wipe to release the fluid. Then apply clean plasters.

Athlete's foot

This fungal infection thrives in places where there are bare, wet feet – especially swimming pools and bathrooms. Look out for:

- itching
- whitening of the skin between the fourth and fifth toes
- skin rubbing off
- patchy thickening of the skin on the sole of the foot

Treat with athlete's foot ointment at once. Be scrupulous about washing and drying your feet, especially after swimming and showers. Change into clean socks daily.

Sprained ankle

A sudden pull or fall can result in a sprained or twisted ankle. The ankle swells and is very painful. Having an X-ray is the only way to be sure the bone is not broken, so you should get medical attention if the pain persists. In the meantime:

- Do not walk on the affected ankle until the pain subsides.
- Raise your ankle and apply a cold compress (an ice pack or a bag of frozen peas is ideal) for at least half an hour or until the swelling is reduced.

- Wrap a bandage securely around the ankle and foot.
- Take painkillers if necessary.
- Once the pain subsides, exercise the foot and ankle gently (see box).

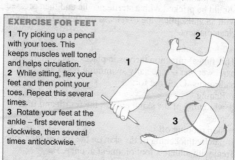

EXERCISE FOR FEET

1 Try picking up a pencil with your toes. This keeps muscles well toned and helps circulation.

2 While sitting, flex your feet and then point your toes. Repeat this several times.

3 Rotate your feet at the ankle – first several times clockwise, then several times anticlockwise.

Most common foot problems can be avoided by:
- wearing well-fitting footwear
- wearing footwear made of natural material that allow sweat to evaporate
- keeping your feet clean and dry
- putting your feet up as often as you can to reduce swelling
- giving yourself a weekly pedicure (see box opposite)
- exercising your feet regularly (see box above)

PEDICURE

A pedicure every week or so keeps your feet in good condition.

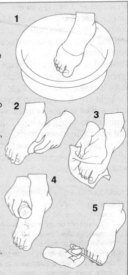

1 Bathe your feet in alternate baths of hot and cold water; this helps relieve tired feet.
2 Rub down calluses or hard skin patches with pumice stone smeared with soap. Do not pare or cut skin away.
3 Dry your feet thoroughly, particularly between the toes, to discourage fungal infections such as athlete's foot.
4 Dust your feet lightly with talcum powder to help prevent sweaty feet; too much will aggravate the problem.
5 Cut your toenails straight across; do not shape or cut them down at the sides, as this will encourage ingrowing.

EYE PROBLEMS

If you wear glasses or contact lenses, take a spare pair with you in case of loss or damage. It might help also to carry a copy of your prescription – although often you will be asked to undergo an examination for replacement glasses whether or not you know your prescription. Even if you normally wear contact lenses, carry a pair of glasses as well as a spare pair of contacts. Your eyes will be under special strains from sun and sand, and you may need to give your eyes a break from contacts.

Protecting eyes from damage Wear sunglasses (prescription if necessary) that will protect your eyes from harmful ultraviolet light. Exposure to strong sunlight can damage your corneas. In mild cases, your eyes will be red and sore; in more severe cases, exposure to strong sunlight can cause blurred vision and intense light sensitivity.

If you plan on doing a lot of swimming, invest in a pair of well-fitting goggles. Both chlorine and salt can irritate your eyes.

REMOVING FOREIGN BODIES FROM THE EYE

- Blinking the eye under water or in a full eyebath will often remove a foreign body.
- A piece of grit on the inside of a lid or near the edge of the cornea can often be picked off with the corner of a folded handkerchief or tissue.
- If the body is not easily located, it may be helpful to roll the upper lid up with a matchstick to see it. This is easier if the victim looks steadily downward while a second person folds the lid.
- If the foreign body remains, get medical attention. Do not persist if the grit seems embedded.
- Never use a needle or other hard pointed object, and never try to remove a foreign body in the centre of the cornea. Scarring here will seriously affect viison.

BACK PROBLEMS

Your back may be under unusual strain while travelling,
especially if you are carrying heavy luggage.

- Use trolleys and hand carts to transport your luggage
  where possible, especially at airports.
- Lighten your load by carrying only what you need
  when on day trips. If you have heavy valuables that
  you don't want to leave in a hotel room, ask about
  the hotel safe (see also pp.147–8).
- Carry a handbag across your shoulders rather than on
  one shoulder.
- If you must carry a lot of gear while out and about,
  use a backpack instead of a hand-held bag.
- Watch your posture; try to keep your back straight,
  your chin up, and your shoulders back.
- Bend your knees and stoop when lifting heavy cases
  rather than bowing from the waist.

RELIEVING BACKACHE

- Apply heat to the back from a hot water bottle or heat lamp.
- Use painkilling drugs such as aspirin, paracetamol or
  ibuprofen for short periods.
- If the pain does not settle in a day or two, consult a doctor.

Exercises

- While sitting or standing, roll your shoulders forward several
  times, then backward several times. Repeat with one shoulder
  at a time.
- While standing, carefully bend to touch your toes, then
  gradually roll your back up until your spine is straight. Keep
  your knees slightly bent throughout.
- Lying on your back or on your side on the floor, bend your
  knees and bring one knee up to your chest. Hold it, then
  release it and bring the other knee up. Repeat several times.

GYNAECOLOGICAL PROBLEMS

Common gynaecological problems can become major
worries if you are faced with unfamiliar doctors,
medical practices and language. Be prepared for these,
even if you have never suffered from them at home.
Early recognition and treatment can help you avoid a
doctor's visit. In all cases, however, if you are unsure of
the cause or if your symptoms persist, do not hesitate to
get medical attention. (Sexually transmitted diseases
are described in Chapter 5).

Cystitis

Cystitis is the term generally used for a collection of
symptoms, usually in women, caused by infections and
inflammation of the bladder and genital area. The
symptoms are frequent urination, pain on urination and
a recurrent or even continuous desire to urinate even
when there is no urine to pass. Because of these
symptoms, it can be particularly annoying when
travelling. As the attack continues, the symptoms
become more severe; there may be increasing
incontinence and often blood in the urine. You may be
able to relieve the early symptoms, but if they persist or
worsen, take a urine sample to be analysed and see a
doctor for antibiotic treatment.

PREVENTING CYSTITIS

- Avoid tight-fitting jeans and trousers.
- Reduce your coffee and alcohol intake.
- Urinate frequently; do not 'hold it in'.
- Keep the genital area clean, and always wipe yourself from
  front to back.
- Always urinate after sexual intercourse.

TREATING CYSTITIS

At the first hint of trouble:

- Drink at least one litre of bottled water.
- Continue to drink as much water – or, if possible, cranberry juice, which research has proved effective – as you can.
- Take a mild painkiller.
- Lie or sit down with two hot water bottles, one against the back, one (wrapped in a towel) high between the legs.
- Use a brand-name treatment (such as Cystemme). If this isn't available, take a teaspoon of bicarbonate of soda in a little water, and repeat each hour for three hours.
- After every urination, wash the skin between anus and vulva and dab it dry. Use the bidet if your hotel has one.

If symptoms persist:

- Pass a urine specimen into a clean, closed container and get medical attention.

Thrush

Thrush is more common among women travelling in the tropics, as heat and humidity encourage the yeast that is normally found in the vagina to grow more than usual. Symptoms include itching and a thick, white discharge.

TREATING THRUSH

- Always wear clean cotton pants.
- Keep the genital area clean, cool and dry. Try to get a hotel with a bidet in the bathroom, and use it.
- Add a cup of vinegar to the bath.
- Place live natural yoghurt inside your vagina (keep it there with a tampon).

If symptoms persist or worsen, see a doctor for antifungal treatment.

FOOD HAZARDS
Food poisoning

The main food hazard encountered by travellers is food poisoning, which can be caused by:

- bacteria. One of the most common is salmonella, found especially in poultry and eggs. Other bacteria form toxins that spread from active infections, such as boils, via the hands of food handlers.
- viruses in food, especially found in shellfish
- naturally occuring poisons in some plants and animals. These are found in some varieties of mushroom and wild berries, and in a few local foods – including cassava, a staple in many African and South American countries, and puffer fish, a Japanese delicacy – when they are undercooked.

Most types of food poisoning have similar symptoms, which occur at any time from half an hour to an hour after eating (many plant poisonings) to two days after consumption (some cases of salmonella, for instance). Symptoms include:

- nausea
- vomiting
- fever
- diarrhoea
- stomach pain
- loss of appetite

Some naturally occurring poisons cause additional symptoms, including:

- a 'floating' feeling and partial paralysis (shellfish poisoning)
- acute vomiting when alcohol is taken (ink-cap mushroom)
- visual hallucinations and acute gastroenteritis ('magic' mushroom)

- numbness of the mouth and throat (ciguatera poisoning, caused by toxins in some fish)

AVOIDING FOOD POISONING

Don't let fear of food poisoning spoil your holiday by preventing you from trying local specialities. Most foods, when properly prepared and thoroughly cooked, will be safe to eat. Nevertheless, taking precautions will minimize your risk of getting ill from contaminated food.

- Follow careful personal hygiene practices and limit yourself to meals in places where you know good hygiene is practised. In general, most restaurants and street stalls that are popular with local people will be reliable.
- Avoid raw eggs and any undercooked, lukewarm or reheated meat dishes.
- Be sure all fruit and vegetables are thoroughly washed.
- Avoid any obviously rotting or mouldy food.
- Do not eat wild berries or mushrooms unless you know they are safe to eat.
- Be wary when travelling where hardship conditions (drought, poverty, etc.) make food scarce and good hygiene difficult.

TREATING FOOD POISONING

Most illnesses caused by food poisoning are not serious and will last only for a few days. In all cases where food poisoning is suspected, avoid solid food but drink a lot of bottled water, as well as rehydrating solution (see p.61). If vomiting and diarrhoea are severe or persistent, or if more serious symptoms such as shock occur (indicated by clammy skin, weak breathing, rapid and weak pulse, dizziness, fainting), get medical attention. In all cases of suspected mushroom poisoning, urgent medical attention is vital.

VOMITING AND CONTRACEPTION

Please bear in mind that vomiting can flush any medication you are on out of your system. So if you are on the Pill, use condoms to minimize the risk of unwanted pregnancy.

Diseases from food

Other food-related health risks for travellers are diseases that are transmitted through food. Food can be contaminated by infected food handlers, by flies, and by larvae and cysts from worms. Diseases transmitted in these ways include cholera, hepatitis A, and diseases caused by worm parasites.

An example of how diseases can be spread through contaminated food is shown in the illustration of the life cycle of the tapeworm.

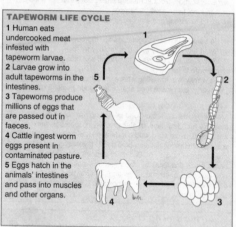

TAPEWORM LIFE CYCLE

1 Human eats undercooked meat infested with tapeworm larvae.

2 Larvae grow into adult tapeworms in the intestines.

3 Tapeworms produce millions of eggs that are passed out in faeces.

4 Cattle ingest worm eggs present in contaminated pasture.

5 Eggs hatch in the animals' intestines and pass into muscles and other organs.

More information on specific diseases appears in Chapter 6.

WATER HAZARDS

Deprived of water, people can survive only for a few days. Most adults need to drink at least two litres (four pints) of clean drinking water every day. Travellers to countries where free, clean tap water is not available must therefore make extra efforts to ensure they have a supply of clean water.

Water-borne diseases

Many diseases are spread through contaminated water, both for drinking and swimming. These include:

- dysentery and polio, which may be contracted from swimming pools containing faecal germs that can resist chlorates for some time or sea water contaminated by sewage
- cholera, typhoid and hepatitis A, which are spread by drinking water contaminated with faecal germs that breed where sanitation is poor
- malaria, which is spread by bites from mosquitoes inhabiting stagnant water
- worms, which may be spread by eating undercooked fish contaminated by tapeworms and flukes, washing in water contaminated by water snails infested with parasites, and swimming in lakes contaminated by worms or the faeces or urine of a person contaminated with liver flukes

An example of how diseases can be spread through water is shown in the illustration overleaf of the life cycle of the blood fluke that causes schistosomiasis (also known as bilharzia).

LIFE CYCLE OF THE BILHARZIA BLOOD FLUKE

1 The microscopic worm is present in water contaminated by the urine or faeces of an infected person. It lives both in the water and in freshwater snails

2 It pushes through the skin of a human host when it comes into contact.

3 It moves to the lungs, diaphragm, liver and portal vein, then to the blood vessels of the pelvis, where it produces eggs.

4 These eggs pass into the large intestine, and are excreted in the urine and faeces, which may once again contaminate water.

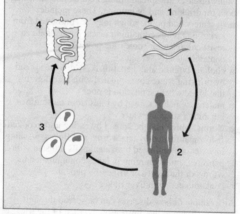

In addition, many illnesses are caused by bathing in waters contaminated by chemical and industrial pollutants. More information on specific diseases appears in Chapter 6.

Drinking water safety rules

- Never drink water direct from a tap unless you are certain it is safe. Bottled mineral water is the safest source of drinking water.
- When buying bottled water, always check that the cap is properly sealed. Bottles of still water may have been refilled from the tap.
- Never drink from lakes, rivers, streams or waterfalls.
- Boil water for five minutes before drinking and cleaning your teeth if you are not sure of the source. Camping gas stoves and portable electric elements with adaptors are useful for this. Cool the water in the container in which it was boiled.
- Filter water through woven cloth or a commercially available filtering bag or device to remove solid organic matter. Filtered water must be disinfected before it is safe.
- Instead of boiling you can disinfect filtered water with chlorine. This kills all living organisms, but strong concentrations are needed to kill amoebic cysts. Use two drops of 4–6 per cent solution to one litre (two pints) of water.
- Avoid ice where you would avoid tapwater. Freezing tapwater won't kill some bacteria.
- Hot drinks, if boiled, are safer than cold drinks made with water from an unknown source.
- Do not drink freshly squeezed fruit juices in countries where worms and dysentery are endemic.
- Collect rainwater in a disinfected container.
- In desert areas, distil pure water by anchoring a plastic sheet and collecting the water that condenses beneath it.

SAFE DRINKING WATER

The table below gives general guidelines on the safety of types of water for consumption.

tap water	generally safe in northern and western Europe and North America. Safe in major cities and tourist centres of South Africa, Australia, New Zealand, Japan, Malaysia, Singapore, the Solomon Islands, Bermuda and Israel, among other countries. Check with a travel agent and specific guidebooks to the area for additional guidance.
bottled water	safe everywhere if in a well-sealed container
rainwater	generally safe everywhere if consumed soon after being collected in a sterile container
river and lake water	generally unsafe, especially if cloudy or obviously polluted

If in doubt about the safety of drinking water, rely on bottled water.

Swimming water safety rules

- Do not swim in rivers, lakes or swimming pools where water-borne diseases may be rife (see Chapter 6 for details of where specific diseases occur).
- Do not swim in rivers and lakes unless you know from a reliable local source that the pollution level is acceptable.
- Check a good beach guide or take local advice before chancing a swim in any coastal waters.
- Avoid swimming pools that look polluted or smell foul.

Polluted beach areas of Europe

Areas of severe coastal pollution for most of the year

SUN HAZARDS
Ultraviolet light

Many people have little idea of the damaging power of radiation from the sun, or of the harmful effects of ultraviolet light. Ultraviolet light causes inflammation of the skin and commonly destroys cells in the outer layer (the epidermis). It also damages the tiny blood vessels underneath the epidermis and affects the elastic protein (collagen) in the skin, making it less elastic. Ultraviolet light can also affect DNA in such a way as to increase your chances of developing one of the three forms of skin cancer (see p.105).

Sunburn

Sunburn is the damaging or destructive effect of ultraviolet light on the skin. Sunburn is more likely in

WHAT IS ULTRAVIOLET LIGHT?

Ultraviolet light is divided arbitrarily into three zones or bands depending on wavelength. Wavelength of light is measured in nanometres (nm).

Waveband	Wavelength
UVA	320–400 nm
UVB	290–320 nm
UVC	100–290 nm

UVA causes tanning and can pass through glass and water and can be reflected. It is, however, a thousand times less active than UVB in causing burning.

UVB is the dangerous one. It causes sunburn, induces tanning and, in excess, may lead to skin cancer. UVB is blocked by ordinary window glass or spectacle glass, but it passes easily through water. It can also be reflected from any light surface. Reflected light can add to the risk of burning.

UVC is nearly all blocked by the ozone layer.

Ultraviolet light is invisible. Most of the dangerous radiation from the sun is filtered out by the atmosphere. This filtering is greatest when the rays pass obliquely through the atmosphere and least when they pass most vertically – as around midday. For this reason, the most dangerous times are the three hours on either side of noon.

people unaccustomed to exposure to bright sunlight and in those with fair skins. Fair-skinned people, especially those with blue eyes and red hair, have less of the skin pigment melanin than average and are thus more susceptible to burning. Young children and babies, especially those with fair skin, are particularly at risk and can burn quickly. Keep babies covered on the beach in hats and t-shirts. Sunburn is, of course, more likely to

occur in people who try to get a tan too quickly.
You might not be aware of sunburn immediately.
Reddening of the skin, which may occur after only 20
minutes' exposure, means inflammation, and this
means damage. It does not appear at once, however, but
is visible after a latent period of anything up to six
hours. It increases to its worst in 10 to 24 hours and

PREVENTING SUNBURN

Damage to skin can be immediate or long term, and both can be
serious. Sunburn on the first day can ruin a holiday, and many
holidays in the sun can affect your appearance and health in the
future. If you must be in the sun, take the following precautions:

- Use a high-factor sunscreen, preferably a waterproof one if
  you will be swimming. For babies and children, use at least a
  25-factor sunscreen. Be sure to cover all exposed skin, and
  reapply frequently.
- Wear a hat, especially on the beach or in other direct sunlight.
- Wear clothes to cover the skin that is most exposed – a t-shirt
  to protect your back, for instance.
- Expose your skin to the sun gradually, starting with no longer
  than 15 minutes a day and increasing the period progressively
  as skin pigmentation builds.

RELIEVING SUNBURN

- Get out of the sun.
- Cool the skin under a cold shower.
- Avoid pressure on the burnt skin.
- In cases of mild sunburn apply witch hazel, natural yoghurt,
  calamine lotion or an 'after-sun' lotion or cream.
- In serious cases of sunburn, if blistering occurs do not pierce
  the blisters; it can lead to secondary infection.
- Use painkillers.
- Seek medical advice if burning is severe.

then settles over the course of two or three days, often with peeling away of the surface layers that have been destroyed.

Even hazy sunshine can burn. If the sun feels hot, ultraviolet light is getting to you. Water, sand and snow all reflect sunlight, so sunburn is more likely on the beach or the ocean and on ski slopes.

HOW TO TELL IF IT IS SAFE TO SUNBATHE

Lie down and mark the places where your head and feet touch the ground. Stand on one of these marks so that your shadow points at the other mark – almost as if you were a human sundial. If your shadow is less than your height (i.e. it falls short of the second mark), be careful about sunbathing: the sun's rays are especially harmful. Stay out only for a short period (not more than 15 minutes), and use a high-factor sunscreen.

Skin damage

Even if you avoid sunburn, all intense sunlight is damaging to your skin and may have permanent undesirable effects. Signs of ageing on the skin are, in fact, nearly all the result of exposure to the sun.

The most important constituent of skin is the protein collagen. In its youthful state this protein is elastic and springy. Ultraviolet light changes collagen, causing it permanently to lose its elasticity and to stretch. The result is wrinkling. Repeated overexposure to sunlight accelerates this ageing process, causing your skin to age prematurely and become yellowed and discoloured.

FEATURES OF TYPES OF SKIN CANCER

Rodent ulcer (basal cell carcinoma)

- a slowly growing, pearly looking hard lump
- small blood vessels visible just below the surface
- raised edges
- dimple in the centre

Squamous carcinoma

- a small, firm lump
- may be an ulcerated (slightly hollowed) patch
- may resemble a wart
- painless
- gradually enlarging

Rodent ulcer

Malignant melanoma

About 50 per cent develop from an existing mole. If a mole or coloured spot starts to change, look out for:

- increasing irregularity of outline
- pain
- becoming raised above the surface
- change in colour, especially sudden darkening
- development of coloured irregularities

- appearance of different shades of brown, grey, pink, red and blue
- development of new 'satellite' moles around the original one
- crumbling
- change in size
- softening
- itching

Skin cancer

Overexposure to ultraviolet light also increases the risk
of skin cancer. The cells of the outer layer of your skin
can be altered so that tumours are more likely to occur.
There are three types – rodent ulcer, squamous
carcinoma and malignant melanoma (see box on
p.105). Be alert to any new marks or moles on your
skin, or changes to existing ones. See a doctor at once.

HEAT HAZARDS

Our bodies have the capacity to adapt to warm climates,
and will do so successfully in most cases. If the body
temperature rises too high, the skin vessels open up,
causing the skin to flush so that heat escapes. In
addition, the evaporation of sweat has a highly efficient
cooling effect. The heat-regulating centres in the brain
monitor the blood temperature and respond at once to
changes. Occasionally, the body doesn't adapt so easily.
Pregnant travellers can be especially vulnerable to
extreme changes in temperature. Take time to
acclimatize in tropical countries. Cover your head in
the sun, walk slowly, and rest often.

Prickly heat

Prickly heat is a skin rash that results from blockage of
the ducts of sweat glands. This occurs in conditions of
high humidity and high temperature, usually in the
tropics. The blockage is thought to be due to excessive
waterlogging of the skin (oedema). Signs of prickly
heat are:

- multiple small, red bumps
- a constant prickling or itching sensation
- occasionally, small blisters

Prickly heat usually settles as you acclimatize to the heat. You will recover more quickly, however, if you make full use of air conditioning and open-air swimming and ensure that your clothing is loose and open so as to encourage evaporation of sweat. Choose natural fibres such as cotton or silk.

Heat cramps

These are due to an excessive loss of sodium (salt) from sweating which isn't adequately replaced. The cramps usually occur after strenuous exercise in hot climates. The onset is often sudden and incapacitating with a hard spasm of the leg, arm or abdominal muscles. Heat cramps can be prevented if you are aware of the danger and take plenty of fluid and salt.

Heat exhaustion

Heat exhaustion occurs when you lose more fluid by sweating than you take in, so there is insufficient fluid

---

PREVENTING ILLNESS CAUSED BY HEAT

There are a number of ways to help your body's natural adapting mechanism:

- Allow yourself to become acclimatized gradually. This can take up to three weeks and involves progressively longer periods of exposure to the heat.
- Alternate periods of activity with periods of rest.
- Avoid strenuous activities, especially at first.
- Take regular and frequent cool baths or showers.
- Avoid heavy food and alcohol.
- Drink at least four litres of clean water per day.
- Replace salt lost by sweating.

to maintain the circulation. Trying to manage on a low water intake is dangerous.

Heat exhaustion is a form of shock. The signs are:

- pale clammy skin
- rapid, very weak pulse
- fatigue
- shallow breathing
- sometimes unconsciousness
- faintness
- headache
- muscle cramps
- nausea

TREATING HEAT EXHAUSTION

The treatment of heat exhaustion is the urgent replacement of fluid, by mouth, if possible, or by intravenous infusion if the victim is unconscious.

- Lay the victim down in a cool place.
- Elevate the legs.
- Give continuous, slow drinks of weak salt water (half a teaspoon of salt to a litre of water) until the condition improves.
- Call a doctor.

Heat stroke

Also known as heat hyperpyrexia, this happens when the temperature-regulating centres in the brain cannot cope with excessive heat production. Heat stroke can occur as a result of excessive activity you are not used to in a very hot climate, but it can also be caused by disease, poisoning or injury to the brain. Other factors that can contribute to the onset of heat stroke include:

- lack of fitness
- use of alcohol and drugs, including over-the-counter cold remedies

- any skin disorder causing an impaired ability to sweat
- too much or too warm clothing

The temperature rises rapidly – up to 39–41°C (102–106°F) – and the condition becomes highly dangerous, even potentially fatal, in a matter of hours from onset.

The early signs may include:
- faintness, dizziness
- rapid pulse
- headache
- dry skin
- absence of sweating
- thirst
- nausea

Later there may be:
- lethargy
- confusion
- agitation
- epileptic-like fits
- coma

Heat stroke is a medical emergency. The rising temperature causes brain damage which worsens with duration and level and, if the victim survives, this damage is often irreversible.

TREATING HEAT STROKE

The aim of treatment is to get the temperature down by any available means.
- The whole body should be immersed in cold water or wrapped in a cold, wet sheet.
- Use fans to supplement the cooling.
- Monitor the temperature continuously and do not allow it to drop below 38° C (101° F) as excess cooling may convert hyperpyrexia to hypothermia.

COLD HAZARDS

Heat always flows from a hot area to a less hot area. In
the case of human beings in cold climates, this usually
means a flow from the person to the environment. It's
essential not so much to keep the cold out but rather to
keep the heat in. Our bodies do not adjust to cold the
way they can to heat, so insulation – from clothing,
body fat and shelter – is vital.

Clothing

Clothing should be layered and not tight. Try to have
well-ventilated outer layers (with openings at the wrists
and neck, for instance) to allow sweat to evaporate.
Remove layers as necessary as body heat rises. Much
heat is lost through the head, so it is important to keep
your head covered. Tuck inner layers into one another
(socks into long underwear, for example) to prevent
strips of bare skin being exposed, but make sure
circulation is not hampered.

Wind chill

The cooling effect of the wind is not always fully
appreciated. The dangers of a particularly low
temperature are increased in proportion to the force of
the wind striking the body. Moving air carries heat
away from the body faster than normal. For this reason,
protection from wind is an important safety factor in
very cold conditions.

Wind can dramatically lower the temperature of the
environment – the amount by which it does so is called
the wind chill factor.

The table opposite shows you how to estimate wind

speed by observing its effect on features of the environment (using the Beaufort Scale), and then how to determine the wind chill factor in Celsius.

WIND CHILL SCALE

Figures in the third column show the number of degrees below the recorded temperature. Use these figures to determine wind chill.

	Wind speed (km/h)	Characteristics	Wind chill factor
	6–12	Wind felt on face	1–4
	13–20	Flag extends	6–16
	21–29	Dust and paper blow about	8–24
	30–39	Small trees sway	10–29
	40–50	Umbrellas are difficult to use	11–36
	51–61	Difficult to stand up	13–38

Making a shelter

If you are forced to remain in the open for any length of time, construct a temporary shelter to help protect you from the elements. Use the natural materials that are available to you. For example:

- Make a windbreaker using branches, rocks and earth (**a**). Cover the shelter with whatever you can find to act as insulation (mud, earth, branches, leaves).
- Build a snow shelter. If possible, dig snow away from around the base of a tree (**b**).
- If there is nothing with which to make shelter, wrap yourself in a sleeping bag or spare blanket (**c**).

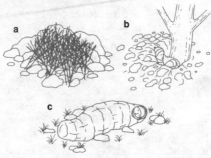

Chilblains

Perhaps the most common cold-weather skin problem is chilblains (perniosis). These are raised, purple-red, round, itchy swellings of the skin on the fingers and toes. They affect mainly very young people, women, and the elderly, and are caused by undue autonomic effect on artery constriction as a response to cold. This interferes with the blood supply to the hands and feet so that they are short of oxygen and nutrition. The result is damage and fluid leakage (oedema).

Chilblains nearly always heal without treatment, but talcum powder relieves the itching. Loose clothing is important, as constriction exacerbates the condition. Keeping hands and feet warm is the best prevention, as well as encouraging good circulation by gentle exercise.

Hypothermia

Heat is produced in the body by the slow burning (oxidation) of food, by movement and by rapidly repeated muscle contractions (shivering). Too rapid a loss of heat from the body because of inadequate insulation and the body temperature may fall below 35°C. This is called hypothermia and it is very dangerous.

You should be aware of the symptoms of hypothermia, and take them as warning signs. Hypothermia can be fatal, and because of its effect on the mind, it is easy to slip gradually into a state from which you are unlikely to recover. Quick action is vital.

Symptoms include:

- coldness of the body in a normally warm area such as the armpits or groin
- pallor
- muscle stiffness
- puffiness of the face
- slow breathing
- slow pulse rate
- listlessness
- ceasing to feel the cold
- indifference
- drowsiness
- confusion
- general swelling of the body

PREVENTING HYPOTHERMIA

The only way to prevent hypothermia is to keep warm.
- Make sure heating is adequate indoors.
- Wear a hat, even indoors if heating is inadequate.
- If possible, have a regular intake of hot food and drinks. Use a thermos to keep liquids hot.
- On outdoor expeditions, carry a sleeping bag or a space blanket with you.

Eventually, coma and cardiac arrest can also occur. Hypothermia can occur indoors or out, and in very cold water. Babies and the elderly – and any particularly frail or thin people – are most at risk of hypothermia indoors. Travellers, however, will be most at risk outdoors – when, for example, walking in very cold climates.

Frostbite

The most extreme result of losing body heat is frostbite. This usually affects the tips of the extremities first – nose, fingers and toes. The damage is caused by the formation of expanding ice crystals in the cells, which freezes the blood vessels and can stop blood flowing to the affected parts. Extreme cold has an anaesthetic effect so freezing can occur without warning. You should be familiar with the features of frostbite. Symptoms include:

- severe pain in the affected area just before freezing, later turning red.
- 'pins and needles' sensation
- white, hard and numb skin, at first
- blisters on thawing

TREATING HYPOTHERMIA

The aim is to warm the body gradually although as quickly as possible. Never assume that a hypothermic victim has died unless this is obvious. Hypothermia protects the brain against lack of oxygen and a person can survive a longer than usual period of cardiac arrest.

- Send for medical help.
- Stop any activity that uses energy.
- Get as much shelter as possible from wind and rain, by, for example, rigging up a cover of some kind.
- Remove wet clothing.
- Put on dry clothing, if available.
- Insulate from the ground with a space blanket, etc.
- Get into a sleeping bag, preferably with someone else to share body heat.
- Cover the head and face and position head down a little.
- Do not rub the affected limbs.

Usually only surface tissue is destroyed, but deep freezing may lead to gangrene, and eventual amputation, of toes, fingers or even limbs. Quick action is necessary to prevent this.

PREVENTING FROSTBITE

As with hypothermia, the only prevention is to keep warm.
● Keep hands and feet well insulated.
● If possible, keep face protected with a scarf or ski mask.
● Be aware of the wind chill factor (see pp.110–11).

TREATING FROSTBITE
● Get medical attention if possible.
● Find shelter from the wind.
● Immerse the affected part in lukewarm water, if available.
● Thaw surface frostbite with your own or another person's body heat.
● Do not rub the affected part with your hands or with snow.
● Do not walk on a foot affected by frostbite.

Recovery from frostbite is often surprisingly good, but the victim usually has persistent local numbness and a greatly increased susceptibility to further cold injury.

4. Keeping safe

In addition to being aware of hazards posed to health by disease and illness, travellers should know about the potential hazards to safety caused by accidents, injury and crime. Knowing the risks and taking precautions are the best way to ensure personal safety.

CHILDREN'S SAFETY

If you are travelling with children, remember that they may be exposed to special dangers.

- If you're in a high-rise hotel, never let them play on balconies or near open windows.
- Explain why they should be careful of stray dogs and cats they will see in the street.
- Warn them not to touch large spiders they may come across while playing.
- Never leave a child in or near water unattended – they can drown very quickly.
- Tell them not to eat or drink anything without asking you first.
- Tell them that the rules about talking to strangers or going off with them are the same as at home – and keep an even closer eye on toddlers than you would at home.

GENERAL WATER SAFETY

Travellers and holidaymakers who do not normally live near water are often unaware of its dangers. Even for experienced water sports enthusiasts, it is important to make use of any information services giving details of

tides, weather forecasts, and details of sea and coastal
conditions if you are planning any recreational
activities on or near the sea. Incoming tides, tidal
waves, high seas and crumbling cliffs make coastlines
dangerous too.

But holidays by or on the sea need not be risky if you
keep the following guidelines in mind:

- Obey coastguards' flag signals. Do not swim if the
  red danger flag is flying. If you know you are colour
  blind, ask which flag is displayed.
- Keep away from cliff edges, which often overhang
  and may crumble. Walk only along marked cliff-top
  paths.
- Do not walk along cliff tops if wind is forecast –
  winds are stronger in high, open places.
- Do not sit beneath overhanging cliffs; you may be hit
  by falling rocks.
- It is best to sea-fish from piers, or hire a boat piloted
  by a local. High waves can sweep you off seaside
  rocks or jetties.
- Bathe only at supervised beaches, if possible, and
  swim in areas where others are swimming and where
  you are in sight of a lifeguard, if there is one.
- Do not swim where people are driving powerboats,
  wet-bikes, or jet-skis. Drivers often fail to see
  swimmers in the water.
- Never leave small children alone, in or out of the
  water.
- Obtain a copy of the tide tables and follow them.
  Walk along a beach and explore caves only when the
  tide is going out. The tide can turn rapidly and

sweep around areas of beach, cutting walkers off. Caves often flood to the roof at high tide.
- Do not scramble over slippery rocks in bare feet. Wear rubber- or rope-soled shoes.
- Inform yourself about tides, currents, water temperatures and possible dangerous sea creatures, such as jellyfish, before swimming in local waters.
- Some beaches become quicksand temporarily as the tide moves in. Talk to the locals and coastguards and find out about local hazards.
- In tropical areas, be careful of treading on spiny or poisonous sea creatures, such as sea anemones or poisonous starfish.
- Never fall asleep on inflatable airbeds. Stay within waist-deep areas and know how far out you are.
- Do not swim on an empty stomach or just after a meal. Both can cause cramps.
- Do not swim around bridges, breakwaters, piers or large rocks. Dangerous currents can occur.
- Learn the word for danger in the language(s) spoken in the area(s), and obey warning signs.

SWIMMING SAFETY

Water sports – including swimming, water-skiing, and scuba diving – are, to many people, an essential part of a holiday in the sun. Swimming, especially, is one of the best forms of exercise for young and old alike. But water can be a danger, and it's important to have a sensible approach to all water sports.

Swimming in the sea

It is important to have a realistic idea of your own

swimming abilities, especially so if you have not been swimming for a long time. Overestimating your state of fitness can be dangerous, so pace yourself. Also remember:

- With each stroke you're getting tired – the further you swim out, the longer you have to swim back to shore.
- It is safer to swim along the shore rather than away from it, but you will be more affected by the waves, especially if they are large.
- Sea tides are more dangerous than most people appreciate, and swimmers can be swept out beyond their ability to return. A current of only one mile per hour is too strong even for most strong and experienced swimmers.
- Don't drink and swim. Alcohol impairs judgement and can cause cramps.

Swimming pools

These, too, have their dangers. The most common cause of injury in swimming pools is alcohol. Drowning in quite small pools is by no means uncommon.

Another danger is diving into shallow water; it is not unknown for people, under the influence of alcohol, to dive into empty pools. The typical injury from this is a broken neck often with such severe damage to the spinal cord that, if the victim survives, he or she is liable to be paralysed from the neck down.

- When diving into a pool, the water needs to be at least 2 m deep. From diving boards and other heights, much deeper water is needed.

SNORKELLING SAFETY

Snorkelling is generally safe as long as your equipment is of good quality, in good order and is properly used. If possible, practise in a swimming pool.

- Use a snorkel tube that is 35 cm in length, with a diameter of 2 cm.
- Make sure that your mask fully covers your nose.
- Ensure that the snorkel mouthpiece is the right size for you. You can relieve mask pressure on your face by blowing out through your nose.
- Do not try and take lots of deep breaths before going underwater in an effort to stay under longer. Take one deep breath and surface as often as you need to.
- Wear a t-shirt to protect your back which will be constantly exposed to the sun.

Snorkelling equipment

SCUBA DIVING SAFETY

Scuba diving presents a fascinating opportunity to view underwater marine life, and it is a popular holiday pastime. It should not, however, be regarded as a casual holiday sport, but as an activity requiring careful training and strict control. It can pose very real dangers, especially for the inexperienced. If you are not a trained diver, you should arrange training – either before you depart on holiday or once you arrive. Such courses usually take about three weeks for full training. People who run scuba-diving facilities are, in general, well aware of the dangers and view the matter responsibly. Properly organized diving centres, whether at home or abroad, will not hire out equipment unless you can produce a certificate of competence or have been trained by them.

If you plan to take up scuba diving, you must be medically fit. There are certain medical conditions that will render you unfit because your body may not be able to adjust to being underwater at depths. These conditions are:

- diabetes
- epilepsy
- persistent middle ear disease
- persistent sinusitis
- eustachian tube problems
- asthma
- bronchitis
- previous lung collapse (pneumothorax)
- previous major head injury
- a history of heart disease

Before you are accepted for scuba training you will have to provide a medical certificate showing that you are free from any of these conditions and are otherwise fit to dive. Assuming you are fit, you should have no problem in getting such a certificate from your GP in the UK. You may find it much harder – and probably more expensive – to get a certificate once you are abroad.

How pressure affects a diver's lungs

Scuba stands for 'self-contained underwater breathing apparatus'. The 'apparatus' consists of an aqualung cylinder containing high-pressure air. The deeper you go, the greater the pressure on the outside of your body. In order to be able to breathe at all, the pressure of the air you breathe from the cylinder has to be constantly regulated to equal the pressure on your chest. At depth, considerable pressures are involved, but because these are balanced by the pressure of the supplied air, you can breathe comfortably.

When you swim back to the surface from great depths, the pressure in your lungs has to be released, so in the course of breathing you release more air than you breathe in. One danger is that panic on ascending can cause you to hold your breath as you rise quickly. The rapid expansion of the compressed air in your chest could cause your lungs to expand and then burst. Compressed air could get into a blood vessel and be carried to the brain.

You will be taught to surface safely, but if you have any of these symptoms after surfacing, get medical help:

- difficulty in breathing
- chest pain
- coughing of blood
- problems with vision
- mental confusion
- muscle weakness
- paralysis
- convulsions
- unconsciousness

Decompression sickness

Another result of the high air pressure necessary when
diving at depth is that much more than the usual
quantity of air becomes dissolved in your blood. The
dissolved oxygen is used by the body, but the inert
nitrogen is not and remains in the blood. When you
come up again, the pressure is lowered and the
dissolved nitrogen has to escape from the blood. If it
does so quickly, as in an emergency ascent from a great
depth, it will appear in the form of bubbles large
enough to block off small arteries.

In mild cases decompression sickness (also known as
'the bends') simply causes pain, felt most often in or
around the joints, but in more serious cases, many
bubbles form in every part of the body. These bubbles
deprive various parts of the body of blood and may, in
consequence, cause:

- fatigue
- skin rashes
- swelling or marbling of the skin
- itchy skin rash
- pain in the abdomen
- destruction of bone

The worst effects occur in the brain and spinal cord.
These include:

- numbness
- muscle weakness
- vertigo
- total paralysis
- loss of bladder or bowel control
- death

In serious cases the victim is taken to a compression
chamber as quickly as possible. A helicopter should be
called to minimize delay. If the affected person is

compressed again, the bubbles dissolve and the flow of
blood is restored. The pressure can then be very slowly
released. Always be aware of the location of the nearest
recompression tank facility.

Decompression sickness can also occur during a flight
immediately following a dive. This is because of the
decreased air pressure inside the aircraft. Wait at least
one day after a dive before flying.

Other problems

Other, less drastic risks posed by scuba diving include
problems with the ears and sinuses because of the
changes in air pressure, and ear infections. Avoid diving
when you have a head cold or infection in the throat or
chest.

WATER-SKIING SAFETY

In water-skiing the dangers mainly involve injury. High
speeds are achieved and sudden upsets are common,
especially with novices. Beginners and experts alike
should keep the following precautions in mind:

- Never consider water-skiing unless you are a good
  swimmer.
- Check your skis regularly for loose components,
  sharp edges and splinters.
- Do not ski in water less than 1 m deep, within
  180 m of a shore, or close to swimmers or surfers.
- Motor-boat propellers can cause horrifying injuries,
  so keep well away from them.
- Hitting water at high speed is like hitting a brick
  wall. You can be struck hard enough to lose
  consciousness, so always wear a life-jacket (**a**) that

will keep your head out of the water.
- Water can spout up from skis and strike your body.
  Wear a wetsuit (**b**) or strong swim suit to protect
  sensitive areas from jets of water.
- Wetsuits also provide the best protection when
  hitting the water and so are preferred for high-speed
  skiing.
- Look out for floating objects. You can suffer serious
  injuries if you hit one.

SAILING SAFETY

Sailing is a water sport that can be enjoyed by both beginners and experts. As with other water sports, however, you should be a good swimmer if you intend to sail. Do not sail alone if you are inexperienced. Check the weather forecast before setting out – if a very strong wind is forecast, change your plans, especially if you have not had much experience sailing. Other points to bear in mind include:

● Always tell someone where you are going and what time you expect to be back. Be sure to inform this person when you do return so that he or she knows not to begin searching for you.

● Get information on weather forecast and tides, and ask locals about rocks and other hazards.

● Make sure you are familiar with emergency procedures and local sailing laws and regulations.

● Wear a life jacket.

● If you capsize, stay with the boat and wait for help.

SURFING SAFETY

You should only consider surfing if you are a good swimmer and are confident swimming in the ocean. Other points to keep in mind include:

● Check to see if any special rules apply. Some beach areas might be off limits to surfers.

● Before starting out, make sure you are insured against the cost of injuring another surfer or swimmer – collisions do happen, especially on crowded beaches.

● If you are hiring a board instead of using your own, make sure it is the right length for you. An expert

can determine this, taking into account your height,
weight and level of expertise.
- Use an ankle leash so that you can be sure to hold on
  to your board while in the water. This is for your
  own and others' safety.
- Avoid areas with swimmers.

Windsurfing

For windsurfing, similar guidelines apply. Good
swimming ability is required; avoidance of others in the
water and ability to react without panic are the most
important points to keep in mind.

FISHING SAFETY

Fishing is not normally a dangerous sport, but you
would be wise to ask at the local tourist office about
local river conditions and any danger spots before
setting out. Listen to local weather forecasts, and dress
for protection against sudden downpours in cool
temperate regions. River anglers need good-quality
waders and waterproofs – and a peaked hat to keep out
the cold. If you are wading, take a wading staff with a
rubber-tipped, weighted end.
If the weather is hot, you will need a sunscreen to
protect your skin – the sun reflects off the water when
you are wading or out in a boat. Wear long sleeves and
a hat, even if you are hot.

Shore fishing

If you are fishing from shore, take the following
precautions:
- Before you set out, ask about current coastal

conditions and take heed of any warnings.
- Do not fish if high winds are forecast.
- Check the times of incoming tides. Some rocks are submerged or cut off at high tide. Incoming tides can and often do throw up high waves that sweep anglers off rocks. They also regularly turn some beaches into quicksand.
- Wear boots with soles that grip. Rocks are often slippery. If you fall you may be unable to climb back up or attract attention, and you could drown when the tide comes in.
- Take care where you stand when fishing from a pier or harbour wall. Some piers have open gratings on which anglers can stand – but they may be swamped by very high waves. Harbour walls have no protection against unusually high waves.

Deep-sea fishing

If you are fishing out at sea, take the following precautions:
- Never go out on a sea-fishing trip alone.
- Charter a boat and skipper. Local people will know the local weather conditions, tides and currents. You can enjoy the sport knowing someone is taking care of your safety.
- Take plenty of food and both warm and cold drinks. Sea-fishing trips often last for 12 hours or more and can be tiring.
- The sun's rays are much stronger at sea, so you will be more at risk of sunburn and dehydration. Drink plenty of fluids, wear a hat when in direct sunlight and use a sunscreen to protect your skin.

- Avoid alcoholic drinks before or during a sea-fishing trip. It is very dangerous to have your judgement impaired while at sea.
- If you are prone to seasickness, take seasickness

REMOVING A FISH HOOK

Even expert anglers can accidently get a fish hook lodged in a finger. If the hook is deeply buried, do not attempt to remove it; instead, wrap the finger and hook carefully and get medical help. If the hook lies just below the surface:

- Grasp the shaft of the hook with pliers (**a**).
- Turn the hook and push the point and barb out through the skin (**b**).
- Cut off the barb close to the skin (**c**).
- Pull out the hook (**d**).
- Clean the wound thoroughly with soap and water.
- See a doctor as soon as possible in order to avoid infection.

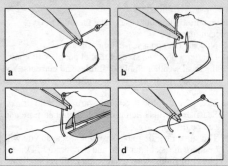

precautions (see p.36) before you set out. Also have
a good breakfast – never go out to sea on an empty
stomach.

- Sea anglers should bear in mind that weather
  conditions out at sea are always rougher than on
  land, and the temperature can be colder. Wear warm
  underwear, and wear several layers of clothing so
  that you can remove layers as you sweat. Also wear
  waterproof boots that grip well, waterproof trousers
  and jacket, and an oiled wool jersey (which repels
  water) and gloves.
- Take spare dry clothing in a waterproof carrier.

RIDING SAFETY

Riding is a worldwide recreation, so just about
wherever you go you will be able to hire a horse.
Beginners will need to go with a guide. Even
experienced riders should be careful not to
overestimate their expertise.

Keep the following points in mind:

- Do not ride alone, especially in unfamiliar terrain.
- Riding over wild open country is completely
  different from riding in a schooling arena. You need
  to know how to control your horse when you
  encounter ditches, hedges, gates and roads.
- Make sure you can control a strange horse before
  you set out. A new rider and unconfined space can
  make a normally docile horse frisky, even in a
  group.
- Don't go too fast too soon. Get to know your horse
  and learn to control it. Walk first until you are sure

of your horse; then increase speed very gradually as you and your horse gain confidence.

- On unaccustomed terrain, always sit well forward, so that the horse's back, neck and head are unencumbered and it is free to balance itself.
- Let your horse choose the safest way down a steep hill.
- Concentrate and keep alert. Bear in mind that anything can frighten a horse, wherever you are. Watch out for low tree branches, rocks, holes and ditches. Some horses are nervous of other animals, too.
- Keep away from traffic if you have never before ridden in traffic. Ask the owner/hirer whether your horse is used to going out with new riders in traffic, and what might cause it to take fright. Only go out on quiet roads. Never go out in traffic on a strange horse alone. Be certain you know the highway code before you go out.
- Check local weather conditions and forecasts, especially about the likelihood of sudden storms.
- Ask at the stables about the local countryside. Find out where you should and should not ride.
- Ask about incoming tides and prevailing winds if you are thinking about beach or cliff-top rides. Do not ride along a beach when the tide is coming in, or along a cliff top in strong winds.
- Wear a hard hat and keep the chin harness done up.
- Do not ride in shorts and a T-shirt – wear trousers and a shirt or jacket in case of a fall.

CYCLING SAFETY

Cycling can be an exciting part of many holidays today. Short day trips are best for travellers of average fitness; longer trips are for those who are very fit with good stamina. As with driving or riding, being in unfamiliar country, with unfamiliar road signs and traffic regulations, can be confusing, so plan any bicycle journeys with this in mind. Basic cycling techniques – including signalling and following traffic rules – apply anywhere you travel.

Also keep in mind the following points:

● Road surfaces can be very poor. You must be alert at all times and spot hazards such as potholes and bumps before you reach them. In general, watch the road surface at least 15 m in front of you.

● Be aware of motorists. Never assume, for instance, that they see you or are abiding by local driving laws.

● Always wear a hard bicycling helmet. If necessary, try to hire one from a bicycle hire shop.

WALKING SAFETY

As a form of exercise, walking is top of the list – and for the traveller, it offers recreation and enjoyment as well. Except for those who have a disabling condition that prevents them from walking with ease, anyone – even the usually sedentary – can use walking as a holiday activity.

Whether hill walking or rambling in the countryside, keep a few precautions in mind:

- Check the weather forecast to avoid getting caught in a storm.
- Wear comfortable shoes that have already been broken in (see pp.86 for general information on footwear).
- Wear layered clothing so that you can remove layers as you sweat.
- Know what time the sun sets and plan your journey accordingly. Walking in the dark, especially in unfamiliar terrain, is dangerous.
- Know your own limitations. Do not be tempted to scale a difficult slope.

HIKING EQUIPMENT

1 hat
2 rucksack containing spare clothing (such as gloves), map, compass, mini first-aid kit, food and water provisions
3 cotton shirt or t-shirt
4 waterproof jacket that is both lightweight and warm
5 comfortable trousers with pockets
6 long, thick socks
7 strong, comfortable walking boots. They should have thick rubber or composition soles with deep grooves that provide cushioning and good grip.

CLIMBING SAFETY

Unlike walking, mountain climbing is a sport requiring
preparation and fitness. Mountain rescue teams are
regularly called on to save people who should never
have got into trouble in the first place. Don't disregard
the advice of local experts. Even experienced climbers
can run into trouble because of unexpected weather
conditions or unfamiliarity with the terrain.

You need to judge not only how difficult the climb is,
but also whether you and your companions are fit and
experienced enough to do it. Take expert advice.

Footwear

Shoes and boots for walking and climbing should be
chosen with care well in advance, and be broken in. The
stresses on your feet in a modest hill climb are
considerable, and may result in foot pain from blisters,
ankle strain or other trauma. Get professional advice
before you spend money on climbing boots.

- For serious walking or climbing, your footwear
  should be fitted under load – the feet spread with the
  extra down-pressure of a rucksack, for example.
  Snug-fitting footwear, unloaded, can be
  uncomfortable when you are carrying a 40-lb. pack.
  Check the fitting of footwear while wearing the kind
  of socks you intend to wear.
- Wash and change your socks daily.
- Keep your toenails short but do not cut into the
  corners, which encourages ingrown toenails.
- In hot weather, or when hill walking, use a skin
  lubricant such as a talcum powder on your feet.
  Apply this after washing and thoroughly drying

them. (See pp.86–9 for general advice on footwear and feet care.)

Mountain sickness

In addition to dangers involving weather and difficult terrain, climbing poses the risk of altitude, or mountain, sickness.

Mountain sickness occurs when you reach high altitudes too quickly. The height at which trouble starts varies from one person to another, but problems may be experienced at altitudes between 3600 m and 5500 m. The reduced atmospheric pressure drives less oxygen into the blood, forcing you to breathe more deeply and more rapidly. This in turn causes you to lose excessive carbon dioxide, and the stimulus to deep breathing is reduced.

Children are more susceptible to mountain sickness than adults because they don't acclimatize to the change in altitude as well. Similarly, those who ascend more quickly, such as travellers in vehicles or airplanes, are more at risk than those who ascend more slowly, such as trekkers.

At about 2200 m the body needs to begin to adapt. The adjustments it makes include:

● deeper breathing
● an increase in the volume of the blood
● an increase in the number of red cells in the blood
● increased excretion of bicarbonate in the urine

Above about 4000 m the normal oxygen supply to the tissues can only be maintained if the heart beats faster so as to pump blood more quickly. These adjustments

EXAMPLES OF HIGH-ALTITUDE DESTINATIONS

Mexico City, Mexico	2300 metres
Addis Ababa, Ethiopia	2408 m
Aspen, Colorado	2410 to 3417 m
La Paz, Bolivia	3577 m
Mont Blanc, France	4807 m summit
Lhasa, Tibet	3597 m
Mt Everest base camp, Nepal	5000 m

are usually effective up to about 5300 m, but above this altitude the amount of oxygen in the blood drops and the capacity for work declines. However well adapted you may be, if you stay above this altitude you must expect certain adverse effects. These are:

- loss of appetite
- loss of weight
- greatly reduced physical capacity
- loss of mental power and impaired judgement
- increased susceptibility to infection
- risk of dangerous mountain sickness

Even the most perfectly adapted person cannot live permanently above about 5500 m.

The symptoms of incipient mountain sickness include:

- breathlessness
- nausea
- dizziness
- a sense of fullness in the chest
- headache
- weakness
- insomnia

MOUNTAIN SICKNESS

Preventing mountain sickness

The key to preventing mountain sickness is to make your ascent gradually.

- If you are climbing, take your time.
- If you are flying or driving to a high-altitude destination to begin climbing, give yourself time to acclimatize after arriving. Depending on the altitude, this might take two or three days.
- If you are trekking over several days, try to spend the nights at a lower altitude and venture higher during the days.
- Rest frequently at high altitudes.
- Get medical advice before taking preventative drugs; some have serious side effects.

Treating mountain sickness

- The most important treatment for anyone suffering symptoms of severe mountain sickness is to return to a lower altitude immediately and get medical attention.
- For anyone suffering symptoms of mild mountain sickness, it is important to stop your ascent and give yourself time to acclimatize.

These symptoms are a warning of the danger of continuing to go higher and a clear indication that time is needed for acclimatization. This may take only two or three days, after which the symptoms usually settle and further ascent is possible.

If you ignore these symptoms and proceed to higher altitudes, the condition may progress to a malignant and highly dangerous phase. In this, the lungs become waterlogged, so that the oxygen intake is severely restricted and blueness of the skin (cyanosis) may develop. Excess fluid in the brain also develops and you are liable to suffer:

- defective vision from bleeding into the retinas
- unsteadiness
- irrational behaviour
- slurred speech
- severe headache
- drowsiness
- behaviour closely resembling intoxication
- coma
- sometimes death

People with these symptoms must be brought down to lower altitudes immediately so that they are automatically supplied with adequate oxygen. Lung and brain oedema can prove fatal unless quickly corrected. *Unless oxygen is available, life can often be saved only by a rapid descent.* Fluid in the lungs is reduced by the use of a drug to increase urinary output, such as Diamox, and brain swelling can be treated with the steroid dexamethasone.

SKIING SAFETY
As millions of people have discovered, skiing can be an exciting form of exercise and recreation. It can also, as everyone knows, be dangerous. Even experienced skiers can have accidents, but most accidents can be avoided by being prepared and being aware. The most important preparation is exercise; skiing is a demanding sport requiring general fitness and stamina.

Are you fit?
Skiing is such an attractive prospect that it can give even normally sedentary people the motivation to get fit. If you are in this group, you would need a minimum of six weeks to reach a safe standard of fitness. Although overall fitness is needed, your leg muscles

need to be in particularly good condition. A typical
exercise programme to prepare for a skiing holiday
might include running, cycling or gym work-outs.
Swimming is excellent, and so is brisk walking,
especially uphill. Many skiing injuries result from a
lack of the necessary muscle power to get yourself out
of trouble. Control over your skis requires more
strength than most beginners realize.

Remember, too, that you may be working at high
altitudes where atmospheric oxygen pressure is lower.
Any amount of exertion will therefore be more difficult
than at sea level.

Practice

In addition to exercise, regular practice, under
professional instruction, on a dry ski slope will help
beginners to get fit and reveal which of your muscles
needs strengthening. Dry slope work will help
beginners to decide the best length of skis for you
(shorter skis are much easier for beginners and are
generally safer) and familiarize you with different kinds
of bindings.

Practice on dry slopes does not, however, do much to
prepare you for the unexpected effects of typical skiing
landscapes with their variety of features and change of
steepness.

Equipment and clothing

Equipment is very expensive, but worth it if you decide
that skiing holidays will be an annual event for you.
Otherwise, hire it. If you're buying equipment, take
specialist advice. If hiring, get your instructor to check

EXERCISES TO HELP STRENGTHEN THE LEGS

1 Leg extensions strengthen the quadriceps muscles (**a**).
2 Hamstring curls strengthen the hamstring muscles (**b**).
3 Side leg raises help strengthen the abductor muscles (**c**) of the thigh.

Embark on a fitness training programme only with your doctor's approval and use gymnasium equipment under the supervision of a qualified instructor.

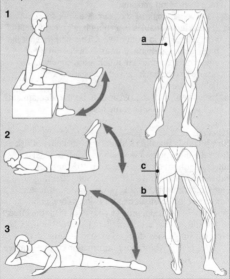

your boots, ski poles and bindings are safe for you.
Ski bindings should give way to prevent injury – your
instructor should check this. Some kinds of bindings
are prone to freeze solid, which can be very dangerous.
Check before you start that all is well in this respect.

Other clothing notes include:
- Keep your head warm. A ski mask also protects the
  face from wind and sun.
- Have a spare pair of socks in case your feet get wet.
- If carrying valuables in a 'bum bag', wear it behind
  you instead of in front of you. This will prevent the
  bag causing abdominal injuries in case of a fall.
  Abdominal injuries are much more common than
  injuries to the back caused by wearing a 'bum bag'
  behind you.
- Layer your clothing. Wear thin, light undergarments,
  and windproof outer garments.

Hazards

Sun hazards for skiers Skiers are especially at risk
from the damaging or destructive effect of solar
ultraviolet light on the skin (see p.102 for more
information on ultraviolet light). Sun reflecting off
snow increases its burning power. Use high-factor
sunscreen lotion on all exposed skin to prevent
sunburn. In addition, protect your eyes from the effects
of the sun and the reflected glare ('snow blindness') by
wearing sunglasses strapped around your head, or
goggles (see p.90 for more information on eye damage
from the sun).

Cold hazards for skiers Be prepared for the cold, which can be heightened by dampness and wind. (See pp.110–16 for information on preventing injury caused by the cold.)

Mountain sickness for skiers For downhill skiers, mountain sickness may be a concern, especially if your body has not had a chance to acclimatize to the high altitude. (See pp.136–9 for more information on preventing and treating mountain sickness.)

Ski lift hazards Beginners are often nervous about getting on and off ski lifts, especially constantly moving drag lifts. Before trying, master at least the elementary skills of managing your skis. Watch carefully how other people do it.

Keep in mind the following points:

- Lifts use considerable mechanical power, and you can be dragged along painfully if you partly get off a drag lift while it is moving, especially if you get hooked on by your clothing.
- Chair lifts are generally easier to manage for the novice, but check whether any part of the route involves greater heights from the ground than you can comfortably tolerate. In the event of a lift failure you may be suspended high in the air for quite long periods and may get very cold.
- Don't even consider jumping off from a height; this can be very dangerous. If you are stuck, remember that the people running the lift are almost as anxious as you are to get it started again.
- Be particularly careful if your downhill route runs across the line of the up-going drag or chair lift. It

ought never to do so, but you may sometimes inadvertently stray away from the piste. This is a dangerous situation and you are as liable to injure other skiers as yourself. Timing is difficult for the beginner, but the alternative may be to get even further away from the piste into dangerous country where you will be alone. In such a case it is often best to take off your skis and cross the line of the ski lift on foot.

Skiing injuries Apart from painful bumps and bruises, the most common injuries are fractures and ligament tears. Most major injuries occur in inexperienced skiers, though even experienced skiers can get careless and lose control. Most injuries are the result of poor judgement or poor technique. Even the most optimistic skier should learn how to shout for help in the local language.

PREVENTING SKIING INJURIES

- Make sure you are fit before starting out.
- Practise controlling the skis.
- Choose the slope difficulty carefully, keeping in mind your true level of ability.
- Stop skiing when you become tired.
- Relax.
- Distribute your weight properly, and keep your weight on the lower ski.
- Keep your knees slightly bent.
- Do not stop to rest in the middle of a piste.
- Do not stray away from the piste, especially when skiing alone.

Avalanche Take the advice of the local experts and never ski away from the pistes, even on a lovely sunny day. Heed warnings and don't go into places where snow and weather conditions make avalanches likely. Get out of the probable path of an avalanche by trying to ski to one side of it. This will require quick thinking and decision-making, especially as you *must* get your skis off if you are caught in an avalanche.

SURVIVING AN AVALANCHE

If you do get caught in an avalanche, you must know what to do, and act quickly, if you are to survive.

- It is sometimes possible to ride an avalanche but you should never try to do this by skiing. If you have enough time, get your skis off, abandon them and, if you are then in the moving snow, spread wide and try to ride it. This is hazardous, as many avalanches contain heavy blocks of snow and ice travelling at different speeds.
- Hang on to at least one ski pole, if you can.
- If you are going to be overtaken by an avalanche, curl up and try to protect your head. Take several deep breaths so as to blow off carbon dioxide and increase the length of time you can survive covered up.
- If you are covered, immediately make an air space by compressing snow sideways. If you don't know which way is above and which below, spit. The force of gravity works inside an avalanche and you will be able to see or hear the direction in which spit falls. Then try to move snow from above you to below. If the snow is soft enough, you may be able to poke upwards with a ski pole to make an air hole, and then work your way out.
- Try not to panic.

PERSONAL SAFETY

Another aspect of keeping safe is protecting yourself
and your belongings from crime and civil disturbance.
Some countries pose greater risks of certain types –
from terrorism, for instance, or civil war. Simply
because a country poses extra security risks, however,
does not mean you must avoid going there; often being
aware of the risks and taking necessary precautions are
enough. Find out before you go if your destination
poses any particular risks and, if so, what precautions
should be taken.The Foreign Office issues up-to-date
travel advisories (See Helplines, pp.245–7).

In general, you should take the same precautions while
travelling that you would at home. If you run into
trouble, go to the police. This may be time consuming,
but it can be important, especially if you have had
valuables stolen and have insurance; to be reimbursed
you must have a police report.

In the car

If you are hiring a car at your destination:

● Insist on being given a map of the area showing
  detailed road information. Study it before you set out
  to familiarize yourself with the area.

● Make sure your car is not marked as a rental (e.g.,
  with stickers identifying the car hire company).

● Ask for directions to your immediate destination;
  specify that you want the safest, not necessarily the
  fastest, route.

● Clarify at the beginning the instructions for returning
  the car. Preferably, arrange to hand over the keys to
  an employee, who can then check that the car is in

good condition and return your deposit or destroy
any deposit credit slip you have left.

Whether driving a hired car or your own vehicle:

- Keep your windows closed or open only a fraction,
  and keep your doors locked – when driving or
  parked. In hot countries, hire a car with air-
  conditioning, if possible.
- Do not pull over to study a map, especially in urban
  areas. If you are lost or unsure of the route, drive to a
  police or petrol station to ask.
- Do not pull over if signalled to do so by another
  driver – except for the police.
- Do not pick up hitchhikers.
- Do not store your valuables in the car. When staying
  at a hotel, transfer all your luggage from the car to
  the hotel (and the hotel's safe, if necessary).

On the train or coach

- If possible, keep your luggage within view. If you
  will be sleeping during the journey, lock your
  luggage to the rack using straps and a padlock.
- If you are storing your luggage in the storage section
  of a coach, padlock it.
- Avoid having your luggage placed on a roof rack of a
  coach.
- Do not accept food or drink from a fellow traveller
  who is unknown to you. It may be drugged.

In the hotel

- Use the hotel's safe – if it has one – to store
  valuables such as jewellery, cameras and passports.
- Lock your room door behind you – both when you
  leave it and when you are inside.

- Leave a light, radio or fan on when you go out for the day or evening to prevent opportunistic thieves.
- Do not open your door to unexpected callers, and always find out who it is. In the middle of the night, do not open your door to *anyone*, even if they claim to be a hotel staff member.

Out and about

Tourists are more at risk from petty crime than natives. Be aware that, when sightseeing, for instance, you will stand out. Minimize this as much as possible; the more you blend in, the less likely it is you'll be targeted.

- If possible, tour with a native, especially when visiting potentially dangerous areas.
- Leave valuables in the hotel (preferably in the hotel's safe), and carry only the cash and cards you need.
- Do not wear attention-drawing clothes or jewellery.
- If you carry a camera, keep it hidden or disguised.
- Carry a handbag in front of you, slung across your chest and shoulders. Place your wallet in a front pocket, preferably one with a secure closure.
- Be alert, and know where you're going. Consulting a map on a street corner makes you an obvious tourist.
- If you are mugged, don't try to resist. Your life is more important than your valuables. In some urban areas, tourists are advised to carry 'mugger money' – a small amount of cash, kept separate from other valuables, with which you readily part if accosted.

5. Sex and the traveller

CONTRACEPTION

Anyone for whom sexual intercourse while abroad is a possibility – even a remote one – should carry contraceptives to prevent unwanted pregnancy. Whatever your normal form of contraception, condoms are also essential to protect against sexually transmitted diseases (STDs) as well (see overleaf). Condoms may be available at your destination, but don't count on it.

> **DIARRHOEA, VOMITING AND THE PILL**
> If you suffer from vomiting or diarrhoea, any medication you are taking may be flushed out of your system. This includes the Pill. So use condoms or other barrier methods of contraception to minimize the risk of unwanted pregnancy.

The morning-after pill

Post-coital contraception, also known as the 'morning-after' pill, can, if available, be used up to 72 hours after intercourse when it is known that a condom has failed or when contraception was not used. It is only available from medical sources, and should be used only with medical advice.

Abortion and RU486

Don't undergo an illegal abortion under any circumstances. Even in countries where abortion is legal and available, the medical facilities may be of considerably lower standard than in the UK. If you are in any doubt about the safety of the medical facilities in the country in which you are travelling, return to the UK before undergoing an abortion.

In some countries (currently only France and the UK), RU486, the so-called abortion pill, is available for use up to nine weeks of pregnancy. It is administered by medical professionals only.

SEXUALLY TRANSMITTED DISEASES (STDs)

Twenty years ago there were effective treatments for all the common STDs. Today that is no longer the case, and the list of STDs is growing. For herpes and AIDS, there is no known cure. Some STDs have become resistant to normal treatment with penicillin. That is why 'safer sex' practices, although not completely effective, are nevertheless essential to prevent the spread of these diseases.

SAFER SEX PRACTICES INCLUDE:

- reducing the number of sex partners
- using a condom (for vaginal, anal and oral sex)
- avoiding sex after contracting an STD until cleared by a doctor
- checking both partners for infection at a special clinic before a sexual relationship begins

---

For all STDs, abstinence (refraining from sexual intercourse) is the only sure means of prevention. Maintaining safer sex practices will, however, greatly minimize the risk.

HIV and AIDS

Acquired immune deficiency syndrome (AIDS) is thought to be caused by the human immune deficiency virus (HIV). The interval between infection with HIV and the first appearance of symptoms can be from one to ten years. During this time, anyone infected with

HIV, even if they show no symptoms, can spread the infection.

Incidence The United States has the highest number of AIDS cases in the developed world, most of which were transmitted through homosexual sex or needle-sharing. In some areas of the world, however (e.g. sub-Saharan Africa), AIDS is now spread as readily by heterosexual as by homosexual activity. In countries where the sex industry is an important aspect of tourism, many prostitutes are infected with HIV, and the number of AIDS cases is growing rapidly.

Do not assume that having unprotected sex while travelling in a certain country is safe because that country has a low AIDS rate. Even in countries where the number of reported AIDS cases is small, HIV infection can be widespread. Always take precautions. No one is immune to the disease.

Common myths about HIV transmission abound. It is important to remember that HIV and AIDS are NOT transmitted by:

- touching, including shaking hands and hugging
- kissing with lips closed
- coughing and sneezing
- objects, including toilet seats, doorknobs and utensils
- swimming pools and saunas
- insects, including mosquitoes

Features of the disease Only a handful of HIV-positive people, out of hundreds of thousands, have apparently failed to develop AIDS after ten years or so. Many HIV-positive people develop AIDS-related complex (ARC), which features, among other problems:

PREVENTING THE SPREAD OF HIV AND AIDS

HIV is spread not only through unsafe sex; other practices, such as needle-sharing by drug users, also pose risks.

- Avoid sexual intercourse (including vaginal, oral and anal) and intimate kissing (where saliva is exchanged) with anyone who has or might have HIV. This includes casual acquaintances, prostitutes, intravenous drug users and anyone whose sexual history is not known to you.

- Practise safer sex. Use a condom.
(see p.150).

- Avoid needles and other instruments (for drug use, medical treatment, ear piercing, tattooing, donating blood, vaccinations, etc.) that you suspect may be contaminated or unsterilized.

- If you regularly travel to Africa or southeast Asia, you should take your own plasma in case you have an accident. Talk to your doctor about this.

- weight loss
- enlarged glands
- diarrhoea
- fever

Other problems include:

- various infections with normally harmless organisms
- internal 'opportunistic' infections such as herpes, shingles, thrush and tuberculosis
- cancers, such as Kaposi's sarcoma
- neurological disorders

Pneumonia is a leading cause of death of AIDS patients.

Treatment Once AIDS develops, death is certain. Although all the various side effects of AIDS can be treated and life can be prolonged, no cure has been found and no effective vaccine has been developed. Eighty per cent of people with AIDS die within two years of diagnosis.

Syphilis

As with all STDs, safer sex practices (especially the use of condoms) can prevent the spread of syphilis.

Features of the disease The first sign is a painless ulcer (a chancre) that appears up to three months after sex with an infected person. It usually appears on the vulva or penis as a small, red, wet area, slightly raised, and *it heals in a matter of weeks*.

The secondary stage starts four to eight weeks after the appearance of the ulcer. The most common feature is a skin rash of circular spots, up to 1 cm in diameter and either rosy pink or coppery red, scattered over the chest, back, abdomen and arms. These spots are painless and not even itchy, and will eventually disappear.

The disappearance of these early signs doesn't mean the syphilis is cured. Leave it untreated, and more serious problems can follow. These can include:

- ballooning and fatal bursting of the major artery of the body
- spinal cord damage affecting walking
- blindness
- incontinence
- impotence
- inability to maintain balance
- personality changes and disorders
- paralysis

Treatment If you suspect you might have contracted syphilis, however long ago, ask for a laboratory test to confirm the diagnosis. Antibiotic therapy is effective.

Gonorrhoea

Gonorrhoea is one of the most common STDs worldwide.

Features of the disease The early signs, which occur anytime from two to ten days after infection, are vaginal and urethral discharge and severe irritation on urination. Women often have no symptoms and may be unaware that they are infected.

Complications include:

- inflammation of the urethra, prostate and testes in men
- damage to fallopian tubes in women
- pelvic inflammation, also in women
- sterility
- arthritis

Treatment A laboratory test is necessary to confirm the diagnosis. Gonorrhoea is successfully treated with antibiotics, though some penicillin-resistant strains exist.

Chlamydial infections

STDs caused by chlamydial organisms include *Lymphogranuloma venereum*, common in tropical countries, and *nonspecific urethritis*, common in the United States.

Features of the disease The symptoms of *Lymphogranuloma venereum* include:

● genital ulcer
● fever
● rash
● aches and pains
● inflamed lymph glands, mainly in the groin

Many of the initial symptoms of nonspecific urethritis are the same as those for gonorrhoea, including discharge and pain on urination. Again, women often experience no symptoms, but the complications for women include:

● partial or total blockage of the fallopian tubes
● sterility
● ectopic pregnancy
● persistent inflammation in the pelvis
● inflammation of the cervix
● constant, dragging abdominal pain, tenderness and fever

Men usually get off more lightly. After the discharge and discomfort on urination have settled, complications are not especially common. They include:

- inflammation of the testicles, often for months or years
- sterility

Treatment In the early stages, chlamydial infections are easily and effectively treated with antibiotics. Once secondary complications have developed, however, treatment is more difficult. Surgery is sometimes necessary in the treatment of chronic pelvic inflammation, and even this may be unsuccessful.

Herpes

Genital herpes is caused by the herpes simplex virus, similar to the type that causes cold sores around the mouth.

Features of the disease The signs of genital herpes appear within a week of infection. They are:

- a red, painful rash on the genitals or surrounding skin
- blisters, later turning to ulcers
- pain on urination
- enlarged and tender glands in the groin
- sometimes slight fever and general illness

About three weeks after the beginning of the attack, the ulcers begin to heal, and the pain usually goes away about two weeks after the rash first appears. About four months after infection, the first recurrence usually appears. This is often preceded, for about two days, by a local tingling sensation with excessive sensitivity of the skin in the areas about to be affected.

Treatment There is no cure for herpes. Once the virus

is established in the body, it is likely to recur again and again.

● Recurrences are often brought on by menstruation, stress, sexual intercourse or other factors. The drug acyclovir, taken by mouth or as an ointment, can cut down the severity and duration of attacks; it is by far the most effective treatment to date.

● Women with herpes may be more prone to developing cervical cancer and should have cervical smears regularly.

● At all times when any blisters or rash are present, the condition is highly infectious; sexual intercourse should be avoided at these times.

Other STDs

The range of diseases transmitted during sexual intercourse is wider than most people realize. Thrush, although not normally considered a sexually transmitted disease, is very commonly spread by sexual intercourse (see p.93 for more on thrush). Other conditions commonly spread in this way include trichomoniasis and genital warts, which are described here, and crab lice, scabies, *Gardnerella vaginalis* infection, hepatitis B (described on pp.163, 166), molluscum contagiosum, chancroid and yaws.

Trichomoniasis ('Trich') *Trichomonas vaginalis is* a one-celled animal parasite. Apart from sex, it can also be transmitted by moist objects such as towels, washcloths and toilet seats.
Features of the disease Symptoms include vaginal discharge that is greenish-yellow or greyish in colour,

thin and foamy (although it may be thicker and whiter if another infection is also present). Other features are:

- itching and soreness of the vagina and vulva
- clusters of raised red spots on the cervix and vaginal walls
- an unpleasant odour

If it spreads to the urinary tract trichomoniasis can cause cystitis; if to the fallopian tubes, infertility. Men carrying it generally have no symptoms. The parasite can live briefly outside the body.

Qualified medical treatment is vital, especially as 'trich' often occurs in conjunction with gonorrhoea. Both partners should be treated. The usual treatment is with oral metronidazole (Flagyl) or tinidazole. Avoid oral metronidazole if you are pregnant, have peptic ulcers or another infection, or have a history of blood or central nervous system disease. Also, do not take alcohol with it. Avoid sexual intercourse until tests show you are clear.

Viral warts Genital warts are caused by a virus that can be transmitted through sexual activity. It occurs worldwide.

Symptoms:

- pink, wart-like growths in the genital and anal areas which may appear up to 18 months after infection

Treatment involves removing the warts surgically or with a drug applied locally, but the warts might recur even after successful treatment.

6. Disease directory

This chapter describes some of the diseases that travellers might encounter. They range from quite common to rare, and from those causing only mild illness to those which can be fatal. Some occur worldwide; others are concentrated in specific risk areas and are a potential danger only to those travelling in such areas. Details about geographical distribution and prevalence and about vaccination options and requirements change frequently, so for the most up-to-date information, contact an immunization service before travelling. These are listed in Helplines, pp.245–7.

CHAGAS' DISEASE

Chagas' disease is an infection caused by trypanosomes, small single-celled organisms that are also responsible for sleeping sickness. The trypanosomes that cause Chagas' disease live in the blood of infected individuals and are spread by insects called 'assassin bugs', whose infected faeces may contaminate bites. The insects live in the walls of adobe and mud huts, as well as in chickens and dogs.
Incidence Chagas' disease occurs only in parts of Central and South America.
Features of the disease Early symptoms include:
- fever
- swelling in area of bite
- swollen lymph glands
- malaise (general feeling of illness)
- rash

These early symptoms may disappear, but long-term problems may develop later and can be fatal. They include heart irregularities and damage, and severe gastrointestinal difficulties.

Treatment Drugs are available, but they may have serious side effects.

Prevention If travelling in rural areas in Central and South America, especially Brazil, try to avoid being bitten. Avoid sleeping in adobe-walled houses; if you cannot, sleep away from walls and use a mosquito net. Insect repellent may minimize the risk of being bitten.

Immunization No vaccine is available.

CHOLERA

Travellers are rarely at risk from cholera. This is an intestinal infection acquired by consuming contaminated water or food, especially shellfish.

Incidence It occurs in areas where sanitation is poor, especially in parts of Africa, Asia, the Middle East and South America.

Features of the disease Symptoms start 1 to 3 days after infection and include:

- abrupt onset of painless but profuse watery diarrhoea
- 'rice-water' stool – clear fluid with flecks of mucus in it.
- vomiting
- severe dehydration from fluid loss
- severe thirst
- weakness
- wrinkling of the skin
- intense cramping muscle pain

Treatment Water and salt replacement is vital to ensure survival and full recovery (see p.61 for details on rehydration solution). Intravenous infusion may be necessary. Antibiotics are effective, but are no substitute for efficient fluid replacement. Recovery follows in 3 to 6 days if the fluid levels in the body can be maintained.

Prevention Avoid eating or drinking anything that has not been boiled or thoroughly cooked.

Immunization A vaccine is available but is not recommended by the World Health Organization and, at the time of writing, was not required for entry into any country. Contact an immunization service (see Helplines, pp.245–7) for up-to-date information on the requirements of specific countries.

DIPHTHERIA

Diphtheria is essentially a throat infection. It is caused by a germ that produces a powerful toxin that travels throughout the body. Spreading in the bloodstream, the toxin can cause serious damage to the heart, the nervous system – causing permanent muscle weakness – or the kidneys.

Incidence Diphtheria is rare in developed countries because of immunization. The death rate among victims is about 10 per cent. In developing countries, notably India, it is much higher.

Features of the disease Symptoms appear 2 to 5 days after infection and include:

- sore throat
- formation of a white membrane in the throat, which

can obstruct breathing
- enlarged lymph nodes in the neck
- headache
- fever
- difficulty in swallowing

Treatment If the diagnosis is made early, antibiotics can clear the germs and antitoxin can be given to neutralize circulating toxin. Delay can be fatal. The membrane that forms in the throat can obstruct the air passages, so an emergency operation is needed to enable the victim to keep breathing.

Prevention Keeping the skin clean can minimize the risk, but because it is also transmitted via airborne particles, precautions are inadequate.

Immunization Diphtheria is included in the routine schedule of immunization for infants in the UK (given in several doses, usually beginning around 2 months). If you have not been immunized, you may be at risk if travelling in developing countries. If in doubt, have a test to determine your immune status.

HEPATITIS A

Hepatitis A is an inflammation of the liver. It is caused by infection with a virus acquired by the ingestion of food or water contaminated with human faeces.

Incidence It occurs worldwide. See overleaf for areas of greatest risk.

Features of the disease Symptoms appear weeks after infection and include:
- total loss of appetite
- loss of energy

- fever
- darkening of the urine
- pale clay-like stools
- yellowing of the skin (jaundice)
- slight enlargement of the liver with tenderness

The acute stage usually settles within 3 to 6 weeks; in previously healthy people it doesn't lead to permanent liver damage.

Treatment There is no specific treatment for any form of viral hepatitis. Drugs and alcohol must be avoided during the acute stage and alcohol avoided for 6 months afterwards.

Prevention Maintain good hygiene and avoid unsafe water and uncooked foods.

Immunization Vaccines against hepatitis A have only recently been developed, but are not yet available everywhere. They are safe and effective and are unlikely to cause side-effects. However, the preventive treatment, gama-globulin – given where the vaccine is not yet available – is injected into a muscle, usually in the buttocks, and is generally rather uncomfortable.

HEPATITIS B

Hepatitis B is also an inflammation of the liver. It is caused by contact with infected blood by, for example, using contaminated needles and other equipment. High-risk groups include intravenous drug users, sexually active gay men, prostitutes and medical workers. It can also be transmitted through blood transfusions using unscreened blood. Tattooing and ear- or body-piercing with contaminated needles are a major cause of hepatitis B.

GEOGRAPHIC DISTRIBUTION OF HEPATITIS A

Hepatitis A is a risk in some areas of the following countries. Check with an immunization service (see Helplines, pp.245–7) to determine if the specific region to which you are travelling is a risk area; if so, immunization is recommended.

Afghanistan	Burundi	Republic	Honduras
Albania	Cambodia	Ecuador	Hong Kong
Algeria	Cameroon	Egypt	India
Angola	Cape Verde	El Salvador	Indonesia
Antigua	Islands	Equatorial	Iran
Antilles	Cayman	Guinea	Iraq
Argentina	Islands	Ethiopia	Israel
Bahamas	Cent. African	Fiji	Ivory Coast
Bahrain	Rep.	Gabon	Jamaica
Bangladesh	Chad	Gambia	Jordan
Barbados	Chile	Ghana	Kenya
Belize	China	Grenada	Kirbati
Benin	Colombia	Guadeloupe	Kuwait
Bermuda	Comoros	Guam	Laos
Bhutan	Congo	Guatemala	Lebanon
Bolivia	Cook Islands	Guiana,	Lesotho
Botswana	Costa Rica	French	Liberia
Brazil	Cuba	Guinea	Libya
Brunei	Djibouti	Guinea Bissau	Madagascar
Burkina Faso	Dominica	Guyana	Malawi
Burma	Dominican	Haiti	Malaysia

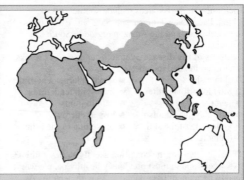

Maldives	Panama	Sao Tomé &	Trinidad &
Mali	Papua New	Principé	Tobago
Martinique	Guinea	Saudi Arabia	Tunisia
Mauritania	Paraguay	Senegal	Turkey
Mauritius	Peru	Seychelles	Tuvalu
Mexico	Philippines	Sierra Leone	Uganda
Mongolia	Pitcairn Island	Singapore	United Arab
Montserrat	Polynesia,	Solomon	Emirates
Morocco	French	Islands	Uruguay
Mozambique	Puerto Rico	Somalia	Vanuatu
Namibia	Qatar	South Africa	Venezuela
Nauru	Reunion	South Korea	Vietnam
Nepal	Islands	Sri Lanka	Virgin
New Caledonia	Rwanda	Sudan	Islands
Nicaragua	Saint Helena	Surinam	West Indies
Niger	Saint Kitts &	Swaziland	Yemen
Nigeria	Nevis	Syria	Zaire
Niue	Saint Lucia	Taiwan	Zambia
North Korea	Saint Vincent &	Tanzania	Zimbabwe
Oman	Grenadines	Thailand	
Pakistan	Samoa	Togo	

Incidence High-risk areas include southeast Asia, China, Papua New Guinea, sub-Saharan Africa, parts of the Caribbean, and the Amazon region in South America.

Features of the disease Symptoms appear 6–12 weeks after infection and include:

- skin rash
- total loss of appetite
- fever
- pale clay-like stools
- yellowing of the skin (jaundice)
- slight enlargement of the liver with tenderness
- pain in joints
- loss of energy
- darkening of the urine

The acute stage of the condition usually settles within 3 to 6 weeks and in most previously healthy people won't lead to permanent liver damage. As with hepatitis A, older people can be at risk during the acute stage. About 5–10 per cent of sufferers will become carriers and may develop complications later on.

Treatment There is no specific treatment for any form of viral hepatitis. Drugs and alcohol must be avoided during the acute stage and alcohol avoided for 6 months afterwards.

Prevention Don't let your skin be broken by any instrument which is not sterilized, or which has been in contact with someone else's blood.

Immunization Vaccination against hepatitis B is safe and effective, but is only recommended for those in high-risk groups.

JAPANESE ENCEPHALITIS

Encephalitis is the inflammation of the tissues of the brain. It is caused by bacteria, viruses and other organisms. Japanese encephalitis is caused by a virus, which is transmitted to humans by mosquitoes.

Incidence It occurs throughout Asia – though it is very rare in Japan and Hong Kong.

Features of the disease Symptoms include:

- fever
- drowsiness
- paralysis
- severe headaches
- seizures
- sometimes coma and death

Treatment There is no treatment available for Japanese encephalitis.

Prevention If you are travelling during the late summer and autumn in northerly tropical areas or the temperate regions of east and southeast Asia, you should minimize the risk of infection by using insect repellents, wearing protective clothing, and sleeping under mosquito screens impregnated with repellents.

Immunization Order vaccines well in advance, since they have to be imported from the East. Few Western travellers contract the disease, but anyone travelling during the monsoon or planning an extended stay in agricultural regions should be vaccinated.

LASSA FEVER

Lassa fever is a rare viral disease discovered in the late 1960s. It is caused by eating food contaminated by rats, but may be spread by contact with the body fluids of infected people, including droplets spread by coughing and sneezing.

Incidence It occurs only in West Africa.
Features of the disease The first symptoms may appear within 1 to 3 weeks of the initial infection. At first they are mild and include a sore throat and tiredness, but they may lead within a few days to:

- fever
- diarrhoea
- inflammation of the throat
- acute pains in the muscles
- ringing in the ears
- general weakness
- vomiting
- death from kidney and heart damage

Treatment Intensive care is required immediately. An early diagnosis is probably the only chance of survival.
Prevention Avoid contact with infectious people. In general this means avoiding the bush areas of high-risk regions.
Immunization No vaccine is available.

LEGIONNAIRES' DISEASE

Legionnaires' disease is a type of pneumonia. It is caused by a form of bacterium that was discovered in 1976. The bacterium inhabits moist places and has often been found in humidifier cooling towers in buildings.
Incidence It can occur worldwide, and travellers are as likely to develop it in the UK as abroad – though the risk is low everywhere.
Features of the disease Flu-like symptoms appear within a week of exposure to droplets from contaminated water systems. They include:

- fever
- chest pains
- diarrhoea
- confusion
- cough
- laboured breathing
- vomiting

Treatment Many people recover after treatment with antibiotics, but susceptible people, especially older people, may die from respiratory failure.

Prevention Careful and regular cleaning of public and household water systems is the only effective means of prevention.

Immunization No vaccine has yet been developed.

LEISHMANIASIS

This is a disease spread by infected insects and animals. It is caused by organisms called *leishmania*, microscopic organisms that live in the blood of rats and dogs. It is transmitted to humans by bites from sandflies, which suck the blood of infected animals.

Incidence There are several forms of leishmaniasis, each occurring in a different geographical region. Cutaneous leishmaniasis occurs in the Middle East, North Africa and Asiatic Russia. Visceral leishmaniasis occurs in India, East Africa and the Mediterranean, as well as parts of South and Central America. Mucosal leishmaniasis and an American form of cutaneous leishmaniasis occur in Central and South America.

Features of the disease Symptoms can occur up to 2 years after infection. Symptoms vary according to the type of leishmaniasis:

Cutaneous leishmaniasis

- Skin sores on the face and arms

Visceral (internal) leishmaniasis
- anaemia
- fever lasting for several days
- enlarged spleen
- weight loss

Mucosal leishmaniasis
- skin ulcer, which quickly heals
- more serious ulcers around the nose and mouth, eventually destroying the tissue

Treatment The skin forms of leishmaniasis often heal without treatment but leave disfiguring scars. Skin and internal forms are easily treated with drugs. Infants and young children especially may die of visceral leishmaniasis if left untreated.

Prevention Do not sit on the ground in semi-desert regions at dawn or dusk, when sandflies bite. Keep children high off the ground at these times, since the insects do not fly high. Sleep under insect nets impregnated with an insecticide containing permethrin. Use insect repellent creams repeatedly and liberally. Watch for symptoms and see a doctor immediately if you suspect infection.

Immunization No vaccine is available.

LYME DISEASE

Lyme disease is a newly discovered disease. It is caused by the spiral bacterium *Borrelia burgdorferi*, which is transmitted by tick bites. The natural host of the ticks seems to be deer, but dogs and other animals can also be infected.

Incidence It occurs throughout the temperate regions of

the world and has been reported in Europe, Australia, the former Soviet republics and China as well as in the USA. It occurs mostly in summer.

Features of the disease The first sign of the disease is a slightly itchy red spot which appears 3 to 30 days after biting and then expands to form a ring. In about half the cases as many as 100 similar rings may appear in a rash that is scattered all over the skin, but most appear in the armpits, groin and thighs. Other early symptoms are flu-like and include:

- fatigue
- fever
- aches in the muscles and joints
- headache
- stiff neck

Several weeks or even months after onset up to 15 per cent of affected people who are not treated develop arthritis or nervous system disorders. These include:

- meningitis
- arthritis
- heart damage
- mental illness
- profound fatigue and weakness which may last for months or years
- muscle weakness
- shingles-like pain in the skin
- encephalitis
- paralysis of various nerves

Treatment If you're on the lookout for the characteristic early skin pattern, you can get immediate blood tests and treatment if necessary. Caught early, Lyme disease responds well to antibiotics. When the disease has progressed, additional treatment is required.

Prevention Avoid tick bites by using insect repellents and wearing long sleeves, trousers and socks when outdoors. Look out for tick bites and especially for circles on your skin, and seek early treatment if you experience symptoms. See p.76 for information on tick removal.

Immunization No vaccine is available.

MALARIA

Malaria is a disease spread by mosquitoes. It causes a million deaths a year, mostly in children. It is also responsible for an immense amount of human suffering and ill health. It is caused by a microscopic parasite called a *plasmodium* that invades red blood cells and liver cells. Thousands of these parasites are injected into the bloodstream by blood-sucking female mosquitoes which have fed on a person actively suffering from the disease.

Incidence It occurs worldwide. Some 100 million cases occur every year. See overleaf for areas of greatest risk.

Features of the disease Symptoms appear any time from 5 days to 1 year after infection and include:

- high fever
- shaking
- headache
- general aches and pains
- chills
- diarrhoea

There are several different types of malaria caused by different species of *plasmodium*. The most obvious difference is in the interval between bouts of fever. This may occur roughly every day, every 2 days or every 3 days.

Falciparum malaria is the most serious. A heavy

infection can block the small blood vessels of the brain and cause grave illness. This parasite also often causes so much red blood cell destruction that the released haemoglobin colours the urine dark red or black – hence the name 'blackwater fever' often given to this form of the disease. This is an indication of kidney damage. The spleen often becomes greatly enlarged and is liable to rupture on injury. Effects of severe falciparum malaria include:

- kidney damage
- liver damage
- convulsions
- anaemia
- coma

Treatment Several drugs are available for treating malaria, including chloroquine, quinine, primaquine, mefloquine and sulphadoxine. People who have had malaria and have been treated and appear to have recovered may develop severe attacks months or years later. This results from parasites breeding in the liver and requires treatment with primaquine.

If you become fevered while abroad or up to a month after returning, it is vital to seek medical attention. If symptoms appear once you are back in a temperate climate, you *must* inform your doctor that you have recently been in a malarial area.

Prevention The real basis of protection is to take a course of antimalarial drug treatment. You must start taking these before travelling. They must be taken for the duration of your trip and continued for several weeks after your return. They are not 100 per cent effective, so it is also important, if travelling in a high-risk area, to avoid mosquito bites as much as possible:

GEOGRAPHIC DISTRIBUTION OF MALARIA

Malaria is a risk in some areas of the following countries. Check with an immunization service (see Helplines, pp.245–7) to determine if the specific region to which you are travelling is a risk area; if so, a course of preventive drug treatment is recommended.

Afghanistan	Cent. African Rep.	Guatemala
Angola	Chad	Guiana, French
Argentina	China	Guinea
Azerbaijan	Colombia	Guinea Bissau
Bangladesh	Comoros	Guyana
Belize	Congo	Haiti
Benin	Costa Rica	Honduras
Bhutan	Djibouti	Hong Kong
Bolivia	Dominican Republic	India
Botswana	Ecuador	Indonesia
Brazil	Egypt	Iran
Burkino Faso	El Salvador	Iraq
Burma	Equatorial Guinea	Ivory Coast
Burundi	Ethiopia	Kenya
Cambodia	Gabon	Laos
Cameroon	Gambia	Liberia
Cape Verde	Ghana	Madagascar

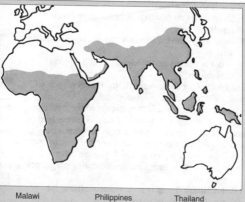

Malawi	Philippines	Thailand
Malaysia	Rwanda	Togo
Mali	Sao Tomé &	Turkey
Mauritania	Principé	Uganda
Mexico	Saudi Arabia	United Arab
Mozambique	Senegal	Emirates
Namibia	Sierra Leone	Vanuatu
Nepal	Solomon Islands	Venezuela
Nicaragua	Somalia	Vietnam
Niger	South Africa	Yemen
Nigeria	Sri Lanka	Zaire
Oman	Sudan	Zambia
Pakistan	Surinam	Zimbabwe
Panama	Swaziland	
Papua New Guinea	Syria	
Paraguay	Tajikistan	
Peru	Tanzania	

- use insect repellent
- sleep under mosquito nets impregnated with repellent
- wear long sleeves, trousers and socks when outdoors after sunset
- avoid perfumes and colognes, which attract mosquitoes

Even following these precautions, however, you will most likely be bitten to some extent.

Some strains of malaria are resistant to the common preventive drugs – in particular chloroquine – so it is essential to get current advice from an immunization service (see Helplines, pp.245–7) on the type of malaria that exists in the region to which you are travelling. Some antimalarial drugs are unsafe during pregnancy (see pp.58–9).

Immunization There is no vaccine available for malaria. Preventive drug treatment is described above.

MARBURG DISEASE

Marburg disease (also known as green monkey disease) and a similar illness called Ebola virus disease are rare viral infections. They are caused by similar viruses, both of which infect certain animals as well as humans. Little is known about which animals harbour the disease and how it is transmitted.

Incidence Outbreaks have occurred in Uganda, the Sudan, Zimbabwe and Zaire.

Features of the disease The first symptoms appear suddenly and include:

- headache
- high fever
- back pain
- eye pain
- chest pain

Later symptoms develop up to a week after onset and include:

- vomiting
- abdominal pains
- diarrhoea
- intestinal bleeding

Many patients die from loss of blood.

Treatment Some people have recovered after intensive care.

Prevention Avoid going to regions where outbreaks have recently occurred. Check with an immunizatin service (see Helplines, pp.245–7) for current information on risk areas.

Immunization No vaccine is available.

MEASLES

Measles is an infectious viral disease that affects mainly children. It is spread by sneezing and coughing.

Incidence It is common worldwide and tends to occur in winter epidemics every 2 years.

Features of the disease Symptoms occur from 8 to 12 days after infection and are normally mild – like those of a cold, plus a characteristic rash. However, severe forms of the disease, featuring severe stomach pains, diarrhoea, and sometimes convulsions, can affect some adults, as well as children. Infections of the ears, lungs, brain tissue, and eyes can arise as complications. The death rate from measles in some poor countries is as high as 20 per cent.

Treatment There is no specific treatment for measles. Recommended measures include isolation, bedrest, fluids, and, if necessary, painkillers to relieve pain and antibiotics to combat secondary infections.

Prevention Young, delicate children should not be taken to areas where there are outbreaks, and vaccination is advisable for older babies and adults.

Immunization A vaccine is available, and is included in the routine schedule of immunization for infants in the UK – usually at about 15 months. Newborn babies have a natural immunity if their mothers have had measles.

MENINGITIS

Meningitis is inflammation of the membranes that cover the brain (the meninges). Viral meningitis can be caused by a variety of germs, most commonly the herpes simplex (cold sore) virus, the chicken pox virus, the polio virus, the mumps virus and a few others. Meningococcal meningitis is caused by various forms of bacteria and is spread by infected airborne particles from coughing and sneezing. It is sometimes called cerebrospinal fever or 'spotted fever' and is more common in children than in adults. It tends to occur in epidemics.

Incidence Viral meningitis occurs worldwide, but the meningococcus variety is especially virulent in Africa (see opposite for areas of greatest risk).

Features of the disease Viral meningitis is often mild, but a severe attack may feature:

- fever
- speech disturbances
- epileptic fits
- headache
- partial loss of the field of vision
- drowsiness sometimes progressing to coma
- paralysis
- double vision
- muscle weakness

GEOGRAPHIC DISTRIBUTION OF MENINGOCOCCAL MENINGITIS

Meningococcal meningitis is a risk in some areas of the following countries. Check with an immunization service (see Helplines, pp.245–7) to determine if the specific region to which you are travelling is a risk area; if so, immunization is recommended.

Benin	Kenya	Senegal
Cameroon	Liberia	Sierra Leone
Cent. African Rep.	Mali	Sudan
Chad	Nepal	Togo
Ethiopia	Niger	Uganda
Gambia	Nigeria	
India	Pakistan	
Ivory Coast	Saudi Arabia	

Most patients survive, often with complete recovery, but some may have residual effects.

Symptoms of meningococcal meningitis are:

- sore throat
- severe headache
- stiff neck
- a rash of red spots on the trunk
- fever
- vomiting

The affected person may become gravely ill within a day of onset and may pass quickly into a state of confusion, drowsiness and coma. Without treatment, death may occur within days or even hours.

Treatment There is no specific treatment for most viral forms, but in the case of herpes meningitis, the drug acyclovir can be valuable. Bacterial (meningococcal) meningitis nearly always responds to quick treatment with antibiotics, leading to full recovery.

Prevention There are no specific precautions to take other than being vaccinated (see below) and avoiding areas where meningococcal outbreaks are occurring.

Immunization Vaccines are available against meningococcal infections, but are only recommended for those going to high-risk areas. They provide protection for 3 years. You may have to be immunized if you are going on a Haj pilgrimage to Mecca; authorities have required vaccination certificates in the past. No vaccines are available for meningococcal type B, which occurs in the UK.

PLAGUE

This disease reached epidemic proportions in medieval Europe; today it is a possible health hazard worldwide.

It is spread by fleas from rats infected with the disease-causing organism.

Incidence It occurs worldwide.

Features of the disease Symptoms appear within 2 days to 1 week of infection and include:

● delirium
● headache
● fever
● swollen lymph glands in the groin or armpit (buboes)
● bleeding under the skin, causing black patches

Treatment Most forms of plague respond to quick treatment with antibiotics.

Prevention It is best prevented by measures to destroy fleas indoors and in domestic animals, and by avoiding rodents (including squirrels) in risk areas. Using insect repellent minimizes the chance of flea bites.

Immunization A vaccine is available, but is not considered necessary for most travellers. It is given to people considered most at risk, including those who work with rodents in risk areas of the world and those on long stays in the rural upland areas of South America, Africa and Asia.

POLIO

Polio (poliomyelitis) is a viral infection of the motor nerves linking the spinal cord to the muscles.

Incidence Polio occurs worldwide, although vaccination has virtually wiped it out in developed countries. It is common in some developing countries.

Features of the disease Polio is usually mild.

Symptoms begin 7 to 14 days after exposure, causing a brief illness with headache, fever and sometimes vomiting, which lasts for a few days and passes with no ill effects.

In more serious cases the central nervous system is affected and there may be:

- severe headache
- progressive muscle weakness
- paralysis of part of the body
- sometimes complete paralysis of breathing
- stiff neck
- high fever

Treatment There is no treatment for poliomyelitis.

Prevention Maintaining good hygiene can minimize the risk of contracting polio, but full immunization is the only sure prevention.

Immunization Polio vaccine is given to infants as part of the routine immunization schedule in the UK (usually starting at around 2 months). Three doses are necessary at intervals of at least 4 weeks, and boosters are necessary every 5 to 10 years for travellers. Anyone who has not been fully vaccinated and is travelling outside northern Europe, North America or Australia and New Zealand should be vaccinated. The vaccine is normally taken by mouth, but can be injected. The injected form is inactivated (all the organisms have been killed); pregnant women and anyone with immune deficiencies (including HIV-positive travellers) should have this vaccine.

RABIES

Rabies is a viral disease, caused by a bite from an infected animal (see p.68 for more information). Bites from infected animals do not always result in the disease developing, but when they do the disease is usually fatal. The virus reaches the nerves in the muscles and travels along them to the brain, damaging the central nervous system.

Incidence Rabies is a serious hazard all over the world except in the UK and a few other countries. It is endemic in Europe. (See overleaf for risk areas.)

Features of the disease The first symptoms appear within 1 to 2 months of the bite and progress rapidly. They include:

- fever
- pains at the site of the infection
- mental disturbances, including anxiety, aggression and delusions and fear of water
- intense throat spasms
- paralysis
- death

Treatment Vigorous cleaning of the wound after the bite or after contamination of a wound or sore with the saliva of an infected animal, followed by regular, repeated post-exposure vaccination, may prevent the virus from reaching the brain. *The disease can usually be prevented if treatment is started within 48 hours of the bite.*

Prevention Avoid contact with wild animals and with street animals in areas where rabies occurs. Do not enter caves inhabited by bats, since the virus can be inhaled. Anyone who will be travelling in countries

GEOGRAPHICAL DISTRIBUTION OF RABIES

Rabies is a possible risk in the following countries if you are planning a long stay and especially if you are likely to be in contact with animals. In addition, there is some risk of rabies in North America, Europe, and the Middle East and the countries of the former USSR.

Afghanistan	Burma	Costa Rica	Guiana,
Algeria	Burundi	Djibouti	French
Angola	Cambodia	Ecuador	Guinea
Argentina	Cameroon	Egypt	Guinea
Bangladesh	Cent. African	El Salvador	Bissau
Belize	Rep.	Equatorial	Guyana
Benin	Chad	Guinea	Honduras
Bhutan	Chile	Ethiopia	India
Bolivia	China	Gabon	Indonesia
Botswana	Colombia	Gambia	Ivory Coast
Brazil	Comoros	Ghana	Kenya
Burkina Faso	Congo	Guatemala	Laos

Lesotho	Namibia	Senegal	Tunisia
Liberia	Nepal	Sierra Leone	Uganda
Libya	Nicaragua	Somalia	Uruguay
Madagascar	Niger	South Africa	Venezuela
Malawi	Nigeria	South Korea	Vietnam
Malaysia	North Korea	Sri Lanka	Zaire
Mali	Pakistan	Sudan	Zambia
Mauritania	Panama	Surinam	Zimbabwe
Mexico	Paraguay	Swaziland	
Mongolia	Peru	Tanzania	
Morocco	Philippines	Thailand	
Mozambique	Rwanda	Togo	

where rabies exists and who will be in contact with
animals should be vaccinated (see below).

Immunization Preventive vaccination is not
recommended for holidays or other short trips unless
you will be in contact with animals. Several different
vaccines are available for people travelling to high-risk
countries for a long stay. The newer tissue vaccines
(HDCSV and PCEC) are safest. Several doses are
needed at weekly intervals. Talk to your doctor about
which vaccine is best for your needs. Some people are
allergic to rabies vaccine and are unable to complete a
course of rabies immunization.

Anyone who has been bitten or licked by an animal in a
rabies area should receive post-exposure vaccination,
which can prevent the disease from developing.

SLEEPING SICKNESS

Sleeping sickness is a tropical disease caused by
microscopic organisms called trypanosomes (which
also cause Chagas' disease). It is spread by the bite of
the tsetse fly, which leaves infected saliva inside the
skin at the site of the bite.

Incidence There are two types, both of which occur in
Africa. In East Africa, the disease is spread primarily
among animals, though it can pass on to humans. In
West and Central Africa, it is spread among people.

Features of the disease In both types, a painful
swelling appears at the site of the bite several days after
the bite. In the type found in West and Central Africa,
this is followed by fever and swollen lymph glands.
Other symptoms can take several months to appear as

the trypanosomes travel from the skin to the brain, where they damage the brain tissue, leading to:

- headache
- abnormal behaviour
- intense tiredness, even in the daytime
- coma
- death

In the type found in East Africa, symptoms develop more quickly – within weeks of infection. Sufferers may die before the infection reaches the brain.

Treatment If the disease is diagnosed promptly it can be effectively treated with drugs. The drugs themselves may be hazardous, however, and in some cases irreversible brain damage has occurred. If left untreated, the disease is fatal.

Prevention The primary preventive measure is to avoid being bitten by tsetse flies. They bite during the day and are attracted to moving vehicles (see pp.74–5 for more on the bites of tsetse flies). Using insect repellent can minimize the risk, as can wearing long sleeves, trousers and socks. Preventive drugs are not reliable.

Immunization No vaccine is available.

SMALLPOX

This disease has been completely eradicated. No vaccines or other preventive measures are needed.

TETANUS

The tetanus germ produces a powerful poison which triggers off the nerves linked to muscles, causing violent muscular contractions. Tetanus is the result of a contaminated open wound: the germs are common in cultivated and manured soil.

Incidence Tetanus is present worldwide.

Features of the disease Symptoms may appear within a week of infection and include:

- difficulty in swallowing
- sore throat
- headache
- fever
- spasm of the chewing muscles (trismus), causing great difficulty in opening the mouth ('lockjaw')
- a snarling, mirthless smile known as the 'risus sardonicus'
- severe stiffness of the limbs
- rigidity of the back muscles
- backwards arching of the back so that the abdomen becomes tight, rigid and board-like
- spasms of contraction repeating every few minutes and increasing in severity and frequency over the course of a week
- death from exhaustion or suffocation in the course of convulsions

Treatment Tetanus can be treated with drugs and hospital care.

Prevention Clean all cuts and wounds thoroughly. If you have not been immunized (see below), take extra precautions to avoid penetrating wounds and bites.

Immunization Tetanus is easily prevented by safe immunization. Boosters are recommended every 10 years; after 5 doses, protection is life-long. Everyone should be immunized, whether travelling or not.

TRACHOMA

Trachoma is an eye infection which causes progressive blindness. It is highly infectious, and in some areas of the world the infection rate in children is 100 per cent. Some 400 million people are affected in certain areas of Africa and Asia. The disease is spread by finger-to-eye contact, flies and contaminated materials (fomites) and occurs among people living in poverty. It persists for many years, causing progressive eye damage.

Travellers are less at risk of suffering severe symptoms than are local populations, who may be weakened by malnutrition and, because of insanitary conditions, may suffer recurring infections. Trachoma presents no problem, even in endemic areas, to those fortunate enough to enjoy a high standard of living, and can be effectively treated.

Incidence Trachoma occurs worldwide, but is prevalent in poor areas.

Features of the disease Symptoms include:

- persistent inflammation of the upper lids and corneas
- curling inward of the lids (entropion)
- deep, penetrating corneal ulcers

Damage caused by the disease, if left untreated, includes:

- scarring of the inner lining of the upper lids
- abrasion of the corneas by the lashes
- damage to and secondary infection of the corneas
- sometimes perforation of the corneas
- spread of infection into the inside of the eye
- permanent destruction of the eyeballs

Treatment The disease is treatable with antibiotics. If you suffer persistent eye inflammation or irritation when travelling or afterwards, see a doctor. Trachoma is rare in temperate climates, but any ophthalmologist will recognize it and provide effective treatment.

Prevention When travelling in developing countries, never share a towel or rub your eyes with unwashed hands. The key to large-scale prevention lies in raising the standards of living and of hygiene.

Immunization There is no vaccine available.

TUBERCULOSIS

Tuberculosis (TB) is an infection spread by coughing. The bacilli affect the lungs (pulmonary tuberculosis) or other parts of the body, such as the lymph nodes (tuberculous adenitis), the skin (scrofula) and the bones. Pulmonary tuberculosis is, in general, caught from other people who cough out tubercle bacilli, while general (systemic) tuberculosis is usually caught from infected milk from cows with bovine tuberculosis.

Incidence TB, once rare in developed countries, is again on the increase, especially among the poor and people with AIDS. It is still very common in many developing countries and is prevalent in sub-Saharan Africa, southeast Asia, Central America and the Middle East.

Features of the disease Symptoms of pulmonary tuberculosis include:
● loss of appetite and weight
● fatigue

- night sweats
- persistent cough
- sputum streaked with blood
- fever

Resulting complications include:

- accumulation of fluid in the pleural cavity and partial collapse of the lung
- occasionally, massive lung haemorrhage
- meningitis

Treatment Tuberculosis is treated with a course of anti-tuberculosis drugs.

Prevention If you plan to be in a risk area for more than a month, confirm your immune status and get vaccinated if you have not been. Other precautions include consuming only pasteurized butter and milk. A drug called isoniazid usually prevents infection from developing into the disease and may be given to people who have been in contact with the disease.

Immunization Most UK residents will have been vaccinated, but check with your doctor. If you plan to stay in a risk area, you may need another. The vaccine becomes effective in 6 weeks.

TYPHOID and PARATYPHOID

Typhoid is a disease of the digestive tract caused by the bacterium *Salmonella typhi*. It is acquired by consuming food or water faecally contaminated with the germ. Paratyphoid is a similar disease transmitted by *Salmonella paratyphi*.

People with the disease pass enormous numbers of

these organisms in their stools, and can continue to do so after recovery. A few remain as typhoid carriers for years and, if they maintain low standards of personal hygiene, these people can infect many others.

The typhoid germ can resist freezing and drying and may be transmitted from faeces to food by flies or other insects, or by direct contamination of food by food handlers. Epidemics have been caused by faecal contamination of tinned meat products. Water supplies are a common source and even ice can carry typhoid. Shellfish may be contaminated by sewage containing infected faeces.

Incidence Typhoid occurs wherever good standards of hygiene are difficult to maintain. Current areas of risk are parts of Central and South America, Africa, the Middle East, and east and southeast Asia.

Features of the disease The first symptoms appear 7 to 14 days after exposure. Typhoid varies in severity from a mild upset lasting a week to a major illness persisting for 2 months.

The symptoms of a fairly severe attack are:

- severe headache
- stomach discomfort
- loss of appetite
- constipation, followed by diarrhoea
- a rash of small, raised, red spots on the front of the chest and abdomen
- fever
- malaise
- a bloated feeling
- enlargement of the liver and spleen
- mental confusion
- delirium

The fever often rises a little higher each day for the first week, so that the temperature chart resembles a stairway, and then flattens. The rash occurs during the second week. In most cases, symptoms begin to subside after 3 weeks and the temperature has usually returned to normal by the end of the fourth week. Sometimes perforation of the intestine and peritonitis result, and the disease can be fatal if not treated.

Treatment Given early diagnosis and proper antibiotic treatment, the outlook is usually excellent. Deaths occur mostly in untreated patients, in the old and debilitated, and in those developing major complications such as peritonitis, severe haemorrhages, and liver and kidney failure.

Prevention Immunization for those travelling to risk areas minimizes the risk but is not completely effective. In general, observe the same precautions used against diarrhoea, dysentery, worm parasites, polio and hepatitis A.

● Remember that the typhoid germ can survive freezing. You can get typhoid from ice cubes in your drinks, so do not assume ice is safe where you would not drink water.

Immunization Immunization is recommended for anyone travelling to risk areas and venturing beyond the usual tourist centres. The newer vaccines are given by injection. Only one dose is needed. An oral vaccine in available, taken in 3 doses.

WORM PARASITES

Many diseases are caused by worm parasites, which are common in the tropics. They are many-celled organisms that range from several millimetres to several metres long. There are various types – the group called

metozoa are intestinal parasites, and are some of the
most common. Many of these can live in the intestines
for years. They are often acquired by travellers to risk
areas; do not be surprised if you find, on your return,
that you have acquired threadworms, for instance.
The most common diseases caused by worm parasites
are described on the following pages.

Schistosomiasis (flatworms)

Schistosomiasis (also called bilharzia) is a disease
caused by schistosomes, a type of blood fluke or
flatworm. These worms live in the blood vessels of the
liver, bladder and digestive system of infected
individuals, causing disorders such as liver and kidney
damage. The disease is contracted by swimming in
lakes and rivers that are infested with schistosome
larvae or with infected snails. (See Chapter 3, *Staying
healthy*, for more information on water hazards and the
life cycle of schistosomes.)

Incidence The disease occurs in the tropics,
particularly in parts of East and West Africa, the
Middle East and Brazil. There are three different types
of schistosomiasis, caused by different varieties of
worm prevalent in different areas.

Features of the disease The first symptoms appear at
the time of infection and include:

- intense itching at the site where the
  worms have penetrated the skin
- local rash

These symptoms may disappear, but weeks or months
later more serious symptoms may arise, including:

- fever
- blood in the stools
- jaundice
- pain in the kidneys (lower back), or on urination
- blood in the urine
- abdominal pain
- liver failure
- kidney failure

Treatment The disease responds well to treatment with drugs – such as praziquantel – which are safe and cause almost no side effects. Surgery may also be needed.

Prevention Avoid swimming and immersion in fresh water (lakes and rivers) when travelling in risk areas. The schistosome larvae cannot survive outside water, so drying yourself quickly after swimming can minimize the risks.

Immunization No vaccine is available.

Roundworms

Roundworms, or nematodes, cause a number of diseases, many of them intestinal. They include ascariasis, enterobiasis, trichuriasis and toxocariasis, all of which are acquired by transmitting worm eggs from contaminated food or hands to the mouth; ancylostomiasis and strongyloidiasis, which enter the skin of bare feet from infested soil; trichinosis, acquired by eating contaminated, undercooked pork; and filariasis, transmitted through insect bites. Several of these are described below.

Ancylostomiasis (hookworm)

These blood-sucking roundworms have small teeth like hooks which they use to attach themselves to the lining of the intestine in infected humans. They cause serious blood loss, often leading to anaemia.

Incidence Hookworm infestation occurs worldwide but is only a major problem in developing countries in the tropics where much of the population goes barefoot and the ground is heavily contaminated with human excreta.

Features of the disease Early symptoms begin once the hookworm larvae have penetrated the skin; usually there is itching at the site and a red rash. In serious cases, the larvae travel to the lungs, leading to pneumonia, or to the intestines, leading to:

- severe anaemia
- abdominal pain
- diarrhoea
- heart failure

Treatment See a doctor for a stool test. Drug treatment is rapid and highly effective.

Prevention Never walk around barefoot in risk areas, even indoors.

Immunization No vaccine is available.

Ascariasis

Ascariasis is caused by a common roundworm and is contracted by eating food contaminated with worm eggs. The worms live in the intestine for about a year, often in large numbers.

Incidence The disease occurs worldwide, with heavy infestations in parts of tropical Africa.

Features of the disease It takes several weeks after infection before any symptoms are likely. Symptoms occur only with very heavy infestations and include:

- vomiting
- nausea
- irritability
- loss of appetite
- stomach discomfort and pain

Treatment Roundworms must be diagnosed with a
stool test. They are easily disposed of using a range of
drugs.

Prevention Contamination can be prevented by careful
attention to hygiene. Wash your hands thoroughly
before putting them to your mouth and before eating.

Immunization No vaccine is available.

Filariasis

Filariasis is a group of diseases which includes
elephantiasis and onchocerciasis, or river blindness.
They are caused by a roundworm whose larvae are
transmitted to humans through bites of infected insects,
including mosquitoes. River blindness is so called
because it is transmitted by black flies that breed near
fast-moving streams.

Incidence The lymphatic type of filariasis, which can
cause elephantiasis, occurs in parts of Asia, Oceania,
Central and South America, and Africa. River blindness
occurs in parts of Central and South America, Africa,
and the Middle East.

Features of the disease Infected individuals can
sometimes have no symptoms of lymphatic filiasis.
Other symptoms, which can recur over long periods,
include:

● fever
● swollen lymph glands
● oedema (swollen hands and feet)

People suffering from chronic and recurrent infection
may develop elephantiasis, in which the testicles or
limbs become grotesquely swollen.

Problems caused by river blindness include, in mild cases, itching skin and, in more severe cases, eye damage and blindness.

Treatment Both types of filariasis respond well to drug treatment if given before the disease has progressed.

Prevention Protect against insect bites by:

- avoiding the outdoors in risk areas at times when the insects are biting
- wearing long sleeves, trousers and socks
- using insect repellent
- sleeping under mosquito nets
- not camping near fast-moving streams in risk areas

Immunization No vaccine is available.

Strongyloidiasis

Strongyloidiasis is caused by infestation by larvae of the *Strongyloides* worm. It is acquired through contact with contaminated soil or sand and leads to intestinal disorders.

Incidence The disease occurs in the tropics, and particularly in the Far East.

Features of the disease Symptoms include a red itchy rash where the worm has penetrated the skin. Infestation, which can last for years, can lead to serious complications, including:

- abdominal pain
- diarrhoea
- creeping and recurring rash
- generalized infection and pneumonia in people with weak immune systems

Treatment Drugs are available to kill the worms.

Prevention Avoid walking barefoot in moist soil and on beaches in risk areas.
Immunization No vaccine is available.

Trichinosis

Trichinosis is a serious disorder caused by a roundworm that infests humans, pigs and rats. It is usually contracted by eating pork contaminated with the worm's larvae.
Incidence Trichinosis is prevalent in Europe and the USA.
Features of the disease Symptoms are only detectable in people infected by large numbers of parasites. They include:

- pain, stiffness and swelling in the infected muscles
- nausea
- vomiting
- fever
- diarrhoea

Treatment See a doctor immediately if you think you have symptoms. Treatment is by anti-inflammatory drugs to relieve symptoms and drugs to kill the roundworm parasite.
Prevention Never eat pork that is not cooked thoroughly.
Immunization No vaccine is available.

Tapeworms

The most common types that affect humans are the pork and beef tapeworm. Infection with tapeworms is caused by eating food (pork, beef or fish) infested with cysts of the tapeworm. (See Chapter 3, *Staying healthy*,

for information on food hazards and the life cycle of
tapeworms.)

Incidence Infestation occurs worldwide, but some areas
pose higher risks.

The beef tapeworm is prevalent in Africa (especially
Ethiopia), South America, and the Middle East. The
fish tapeworm (a less common type) occurs in some
parts of Europe, Africa and South America.

Tapeworm infestation is more common in areas where
procedures for meat inspection and sewage disposal are
inadequate.

Features of the disease Tapeworm infestation rarely
causes significant problems, but symptoms can include:

- abdominal pain
- diarrhoea
- worms in stools

If the disease goes untreated, however, pork tapeworm
larvae can somtimes spread throughout the body and
lead to cysticercosis, which can cause muscle pains,
epilepsy, and even death.

Treatment Medical attention is necessary. Drugs to kill
the worms are highly effective.

Prevention The most important preventive measure is
to avoid eating raw or undercooked meat and fish, even
where it is considered a delicacy.

Immunization No vaccine is available.

YELLOW FEVER

Yellow fever is a viral disease transmitted by mosquito
bites. The reservoir of infection is believed to be the
'canopy' monkeys who inhabit the tops of trees.
Mosquitoes occasionally transmit the disease from

these monkeys to a forest worker who returns to a town and starts an epidemic.

Incidence Yellow fever occurs only in the tropical rainforests across Central Africa and in South and Central America.

Features of the disease The disease may be mild and over in 3 days, but it is often a severe and dangerous illness.

Symptoms appear up to a week after infection and include:

- high fever
- severe headache
- nausea
- bleeding from the nose and gums
- a slow pulse rate
- general aches and pains
- vomiting
- black stools

Complications that develop later include:

- liver damage
- vomiting of blood
- yellowing of the skin (jaundice)
- kidney damage and failure
- intestinal bleeding
- agitation
- delirium
- severe bleeding from the bowel and uterus
- sometimes coma and death

Treatment There is no specific treatment for the disease, only for the complications that arise from it. Mortality varies from 5 to 10 per cent. Those who recover are immune for life.

Prevention Vaccination provides protection for at least 10 years.

Immunization If you are visiting yellow fever areas it is essential that you are immunized. *Infants, pregnant*

GEOGRAPHICAL DISTRIBUTION OF YELLOW FEVER

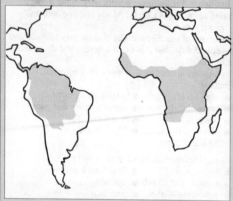

Yellow fever occurs in parts of the following countries. If travelling to one of these countries, consult an immunization service (see Helplines, pp.245–7) to determine if the specific region to which you are travelling is a high-risk area.

Bolivia	Guinea Bissau	Sierra Leone
Brazil	Guyana	Somalia
Burundi	Kenya	Sudan
Colombia	Namibia	Surinam
Ecuador	Nigeria	Tanzania
Equatorial Guinea	Panama	Uganda
Ethiopia	Peru	Venezuela
Gambia	Sao Tomé &	Zambia
Guinea	Principé	

In addition to the risk present in regions within the countries listed opposite, there is a very low risk of contracting the disease if you travel to parts of Central America, North and South Africa, the Middle East, and southern and southeast Asia.

At the time of writing, an official certificate of protection against yellow fever is required for entry to:

Benin	Congo	Mali
Burkina Faso	Gabon	Niger
Cameroon	Ghana	Rwanda
Cent. African Rep.	Guiana, French	Senegal
Chad	Ivory Coast	Togo
	Liberia	Zaire

Also, many countries require you to provide an official certificate of protection if you have passed through or are travelling from an area where the disease is present (although you should already have been vaccinated if travelling to any of the countries listed opposite). Consult an immunization service (see Helplines, pp.245–7) for more information.

women and anyone with suppressed immune systems should avoid high-risk areas if possible because the vaccine itself can be hazardous. You may need a vaccination certificate to be allowed entry to some countries (see previous page). Vaccination requirements vary from year to year, as the disease tends to occur in epidemics, so get up-to-date information before travelling (see Helplines, pp.245–7).

7. Medical treatment abroad

Medical treatment abroad is expensive. Medical insurance (see pp.26–7) must be high on your list of priorities when preparing for a trip abroad, however short your stay.

In some countries, a doctor's visit plus any X-rays, tests and drugs you may need can cost upwards of £100. If you need hospital treatment or surgery, the bills can run to thousands of pounds. Although the UK has reciprocal arrangements for medical treatment with European Economic Area (EEA) member countries[*] and many others, you often have to pay at the time and claim a refund later. Sometimes the refunds are only partial – you still have to pay part of the cost. Such arrangements never include the cost of transporting you home if you need to be repatriated while ill.

Notes for pregnant travellers

If you are pregnant and you fall ill while abroad, fast repatriation under your medical insurance scheme is the best action if you cannot find good medical care. In addition:

- Insist on injections using only sterile needles and syringes from your own first-aid kit (see pp.30–1).
- Refuse drug treatment, including analgesics, unless

[*] The EEA consists of EC member states (Belgium, Denmark, France, Germany, Gibraltar, Greece, the Irish Republic, Italy, Luxembourg, the Netherlands, Portugal, Spain and the UK) plus Austria, Finland, Iceland, Norway and Sweden.

you are certain the drugs will not harm a fetus.
● Do not accept treatment with tetracycline antibiotics, which can harm a developing child.

TREATMENT IN EEA COUNTRIES

If you are a citizen of an EEA member country and are normally resident in the UK, you and your dependants are entitled to free or reduced-cost emergency medical treatment when travelling within the EEA. To claim this, you must have form E111.

Non-EEA citizens resident in the UK may be covered for emergency medical treatment in Iceland and Sweden under separate reciprocal arrangements. These do not require form E111, but you must produce your NHS card when seeking treatment.

If you are still in the UK, ask at a post office for the application form CM1 and the E111. Fill in both forms and hand them in at the post office. Form E111 will be stamped and returned to you. Some countries require the form and a photocopy. Take two photocopies; leave

---

ABOUT FORM E111:
● It is valid for medical treatment in EEA countries only.
● It is valid indefinitely.
● It is valid for emergency treatment only.
● It is valid for all EEA citizens who are resident in the UK.
● It is valid for refugees and stateless people who are resident in the UK.
● It covers only short stays abroad in the EEA.
● It **never** covers the cost of flying you back to the UK.
● It does **not** cover medical costs if you are visiting a border area and are taken across the border to a non-EEA country for emergency treatment.

one photocopy at home and keep the form and the other copy with your passport and proof of residency, such as a driving licence.

If you are already abroad and you are likely to be there for more than a week, claim form E111 by writing to: DSS Benefits Agency, Overseas Benefits Directorate (MED), Longbenton, Newcastle-upon-Tyne, NE98 1YX. In Northern Ireland, write to: Social Security Agency, Overseas Branch, Commonwealth House, 35 Castle Street, Belfast BT1 1GU. The form will be sent to you.

If you go abroad specifically for medical treatment, you will need form E112, which will not be issued automatically but requires authorization from the Department of Health. Unless you have form E112, you will have to pay for treatment you receive while abroad. To obtain form E112, fill in form E111 and attach a letter explaining why you need treatment abroad. Send the completed form and letter to your local district health authority/board requesting that they agree to meet the cost and that they forward your application with your agreement to the Department of Health, International Relations Unit, Room 518, Richmond House, 79 Whitehall, London SW1A 2NS.

Remember the following points:
- Each member state provides services to visitors on the same terms as it provides services to its own people.
- In the poorer EEA member countries, relatively few doctors may be registered under the state health care schemes. You may have to travel some distance to

visit one, and there may be a long wait in a crowded
waiting room.

- You may be entitled only to treatment in public wards
  in state hospitals, and these may also be crowded.
- You may be charged for tests, X-rays and
  physiotherapy.
- Dental services under some state schemes are very
  limited and you are unlikely to be treated free of
  charge or be entitled to a refund.
- You must claim refunds from the sickness insurance
  office of the country in which you were treated. You
  can do this by post or in person; details are given in
  the country listings that follow. Do not wait until you
  return to the UK to claim your refund if at all
  possible; you may have a longer wait.
- There are likely to be long waits in the sickness
  insurance offices.
- You may also find it difficult in some countries to
  claim a refund if you do not have all the required
  documents, receipts and stamps.
- Refunds, if granted, often take some time to process.
  In some countries, such as France, your refund is
  sent to your home address in the UK; you do not
  receive a refund while still abroad.
- *Refunds may cover only part of the cost of treatment,
  in which case you are expected to pay the remainder.*
- You will have to bear the cost of being flown back to
  the UK, if necessary.

A medical insurance policy, for any length of stay, will
ensure that you get the treatment you need at no cost to
you, and will save an immense amount of time.

Obtaining refunds in the UK

Always try to obtain any refunds due to you before returning to the UK. If you could not obtain a refund in the country in which you received treatment, you may be able to obtain it once you return, but the wait is likely to be longer because funds come not from the NHS but from the country supplying treatment.

To obtain a refund once you return to the UK, enclose the relevant documents and receipts (see individual countries in the listing on the following pages) and write to:

>   DSS Benefits Agency
>   Overseas Benefits Directorate (MED)
>   Longbenton
>   Newcastle-upon-Tyne NE98 1YX

In Northern Ireland, write to:

>   Department of Health and Social Services
>   General Medical and Ophthalmic Services Branch
>   Room 909, Dundonald House
>   Upper Newtownards
>   Belfast BT4 3TL

Alternative/complementary medicine

Many doctors in France and other EEA countries specialize in homeopathic and other complementary medical systems. Your hotel, the British Embassy, or the local town hall may be able to give you the names of specialist doctors and therapists. Such treatment will not be covered under the E111 arrangements, and you will have to pay in full. Before going abroad, you should check with the DSS for specific arrangements with the country to which you are travelling. Specialists in the various complementary medical disciplines also practise in poor countries outside the EEA. But again, outside the larger towns these practitioners are often the only medical help available, and their services are fully in demand by the local population. Unless you feel you need urgent help, it would be better to wait and consult a specialist when you return home.

EEA countries

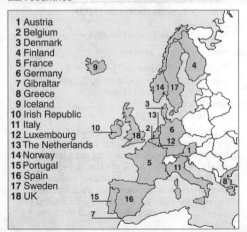

1 Austria
2 Belgium
3 Denmark
4 Finland
5 France
6 Germany
7 Gibraltar
8 Greece
9 Iceland
10 Irish Republic
11 Italy
12 Luxembourg
13 The Netherlands
14 Norway
15 Portugal
16 Spain
17 Sweden
18 UK

AUSTRIA

UK nationals on temporary visits to Austria do not need to submit an E111 to obtain treatment; a British passport is sufficient. Other EEA nationals resident in the UK do need form E111.

Consulting a doctor or dentist

You must first contact the Regional Health Insurance Office to obtain agreement that treatment is required. You will be given a voucher and the names and addresses of medical practitioners.

Prescriptions

Take your prescription to a pharmacy. You will be charged part of the cost of each medicine.

Hospital treatment

- You can be treated as an out-patient in a hospital casualty ward.
- If you must be admitted and treated as an in-patient, a doctor will refer you to a public hospital and give you an admission voucher to submit at the hospital.
- When you must be admitted as an emergency, give your passport to the hospital administration; they will determine that you are eligible.
- You must pay a small daily charge for the first 28 days in hospital.

Regional Health Insurance Offices

For information, addresses of doctors, vouchers and refunds, you must go to the Regional Health Insurance Office (*Gebietskrankenkasse*) responsible for the area in which you are staying.

Refunds

If you receive private treatment, you may be able to obtain a refund from the Regional Health Insurance

Office for part of the cost, normally up to the amount that would have been refunded for treatment in a public hospital.

BELGIUM

When requesting treatment or cashing a prescription, show your form E111.

Consulting a doctor or dentist

Go to any doctor or dentist for treatment. Pay in full and ask for a receipt on the official form (*Attestation de soins donnés/Getuigschrift voor verstrekte hulp*).

Prescriptions

Take your prescription to a dispensing chemist (*pharmacie*). Pay in full and get a receipt; also ask for your copy of the prescription with the official stamp.

Hospital treatment

- If you are taken to hospital, give form E111 to the hospital administration and ask them to obtain a certificate from the Belgian sickness insurance office stating that part of the cost will be paid.
- If possible, take your E111 to a sickness insurance office first and explain why you need treatment. Ask them to recommend a reasonably priced hospital, and also request a certificate authorizing part-payment.

Sickness insurance offices

Caisse auxiliaire d'assurance maladie-invalidité/Hulpkas voor Ziekte-en Invaliditeitsverzekering
12 Boulevard St Lazare/St Lazaruslaan 12, 1210 Brussels

There are offices in the regional capitals: Bruges, Ghent, Antwerp, Mons, Limburg, Hasselt, Liege, Namur; and local sickness fund offices (*Mutualité/Ziekenfonds*) in other towns.

Refunds

About 75 per cent of the costs of treatment and approved drugs will be refunded. If you cannot obtain a refund abroad, keep your official form for claiming in the UK.

DENMARK

Consulting a doctor or dentist

You can go to any doctor or dentist registered with the Danish Public Health Service for treatment. Show a British passport or form E111. You may be given medical treatment free of charge, and dental treatment at a reduced cost. Ask for a receipt for any payments that you make.

Prescriptions

Take your prescription to a dispensing chemist and show your passport or form E111. You should be charged a reduced price for approved prescribed medicines. If the chemist will not agree to a reduction, pay in full, ask for a receipt, and claim a refund from the local council. *The first 800 kroner of the bill will not be refunded.*

Hospital treatment

- If you are taken to hospital, give form E111 to the hospital administration and ask them to arrange free treatment.
- If a doctor recommends hospital treatment, he or she will arrange it for you and it will be free.

Sickness insurance offices

There are local council Social and Health Departments (*Kommunens social – og sundhedsforvaltning*) in all areas.

Refunds

Local council offices will refund costs for medical treatment and part of the costs for dental treatment and prescribed medicines. Show your passport or form E111 and give them your receipts.

FINLAND

UK nationals on temporary visits to Finland do not need to submit an E111 to obtain treatment; a British passport is sufficient. Other EEA nationals resident in the UK do need form E111.

Consulting a doctor or dentist

Go to a municipal health centre and show your form E111 (or passport if a UK national).

- For medical treatment, depending on the municipality, you will be treated either free of charge or for a standard fee, which is not refundable.
- For emergency dental treatment, you will be charged a standard fee.

Prescriptions

Take your prescription to a pharmacy. You will be charged the full amount for each medicine, but you can obtain a refund of between 40 per cent and 100 per cent. Keep your receipts.

Hospital treatment

- For non-emergencies, a doctor will refer you to a public hospital. You must show your form E111 (or passport) to the hospital administration.

● In an emergency, you can be treated at the nearest public hospital without first consulting a doctor.

Sickness insurance offices

For information, go to the office of the Sickness Insurance Department (*Kansanelakaitoksen Paikallistoimisto – KELA*) for the local area in which you are staying.

Refunds

Refunds are not paid on the standard fee charged for medical and dental treatment at municipal health centres. For private treatment, you may obtain a refund of about 60 per cent of a predetermined set fee, but you will not be refunded the private fee. Prescription drugs are refunded at 40–100 per cent.

You must submit receipts with all refund claims. To obtain a refund, go to your local KELA or write:

> Kanseanelakelaitos
> Sosiaaliturvasopmukset
> PO Box 450
> 00101 Helsinki
> Finland

Note that all claims for refunds must be submitted within six months of original payment.

FRANCE

When requesting treatment or cashing a prescription show form E111. Be sure to obtain *all* the necessary forms, receipts, signatures, stamps, etc. as detailed below. Refunds will not be granted without them.

Consulting a doctor or dentist

Go to any doctor or dentist registered with the French medical insurance scheme (*conventionne)* for treatment.

Pay in full and ask for a signed statement (*feuille de soins*) of treatment given and fee paid.

Prescriptions

Take your prescription to a dispensing chemist (*pharmacie*). The chemist will give you back your prescription. Attach it to the doctor's statement of treatment. Pull the *vignettes* (price stickers) off the medicines bottles and packets, and stick them on the *feuille de soins* in the place marked.

Hospital treatment

● Ask a doctor to issue you with a certificate (*attestation*) for admission to an approved hospital, or go to a hospital recommended by a sickness insurance office and ask for a certificate. Give form E111 to the hospital administration and ask them to send it with a notice of admission form (*Avis d'admission –prise en charge*) to the local sickness insurance office, or send it yourself. The office will pay a proportion, usually 80 per cent or more, to the hospital and you must pay the balance, plus a fixed daily charge.

● If you are treated in a hospital out-patient department, you must pay, ask for a *feuille de soins,* and claim a refund.

Sickness insurance offices

Caisses Primaires d'Assurance-Maladie de Paris, Service des Relations Internationales, 173-175 rue de Bercy, 75586 Paris Cedex 12. Tel 42-46-12-53.

There are Caisses Primaires d'Assurance-Maladie in all major towns and districts of France.

Refunds

About 70 per cent of standard medical and dental fees is refunded, as is about 35–65 per cent of the cost of most prescribed medicines. Before you leave France, sign and date the *feuille de soins* and send it with your prescription and form E111 to the local sickness insurance office. A notice of the amount to be refunded will be sent to your home, followed by the refund. If you cannot put in a claim for a refund while abroad, keep your *feuille de soins* and drug price sticker for claiming in the UK.

GERMANY

Members of the British forces staioned in Germany (and their dependants) are not covered for medical treatment under EEA arrangements. Any treatment which cannot be provided by Service facilities in Germany must be paid for by the patient. In such cases, no refunds are available.

Consulting a doctor or dentist

- Go to a local sickness fund office, show your form E111, and ask for a certificate (*Krankenshein*) entitling you to free medical treatment. If you go to a doctor or dentist registered under the sickness fund scheme and show your certificate, you will receive free treatment.

- If you cannot go to the office first, see a doctor who is registered under the sickness fund scheme (this will be indicated on the name-plate outside the surgery). Show your form E111. If you have to pay, ask for an itemized receipt. Go to the local sickness fund office in the next 10 days, and ask for a

certificate of entitlement. Take it with your bill and
receipt to the doctor, who will refund your fee.

Prescriptions

Take your prescription to any dispensing chemist.
You may have to pay part of the cost of prescribed
medicines and the full cost of some medicines.

Hospital treatment

- If you are taken to hospital in an emergency, give
  form E111 to the hospital administration and ask
  them to obtain a certificate
  (*Kostenübernahmeschein*) entitling you to free
  treatment in a public ward.
- If a doctor recommends hospital treatment he or she
  will give you a statement (*Verordnung von
  Krankenhauspflege*). Take it to the local sickness
  fund office. If they decide you need immediate
  treatment, they will give you a certificate
  (*Kostenübernahmeschein*). Give it to the hospital
  administration. You have to pay a small daily
  hospital charge for the first 14 days. If the sickness
  fund office says you do not need immediate treatment you may still ask to be admitted to hospital, but
  you will have to pay and cannot claim a refund.

Sickness fund offices

- Allgemeine Ortskrankenkassen (AOK) offices exist
  in all areas in the former West Germany and are open
  from Monday to Friday.
- AOK offices have not yet been opened throughout
  the former East Germany. Ask at the local town hall
  (*Rathaus*) or police station (*Polizei*) for the district
  administrative organization (*Kreisverwaltung der
  Sozialversicherung*).

Refunds

Refunds are only available if you have had to pay for treatment by a doctor registered under the sickness fund scheme (see opposite). In such cases, 100 per cent of the costs are refunded by the doctor who treated you.

GIBRALTAR

UK residents staying for up to 30 days are treated free or at a reduced cost. Show your passport or form E111.

Consulting a doctor or dentist

● Free medical treatment is available at the Health Centre under the local Medical Scheme. You will have to pay a charge if you call a doctor out.
● Emergency dental treatment is available for a small charge at the Casemates Health Centre during weekday working hours.

Prescriptions

You pay a small charge for each item of medicine prescribed under the Medical Scheme.

Hospital treatment

Ask to be admitted to the free public ward at St Bernard's Hospital.

Information centres

Gibraltar Health Authority, St Bernard's Hospital, and the Casemates Health Centre will answer enquiries.

Refunds

Refunds are not paid as most treatment is free.

GREECE

Consulting a doctor or dentist

You can only get free treatment if you go to a local Social Insurance Institute (IKA) and show form E111 and your passport. You are given a health services book and can receive free treatment and consultation by any clinic, doctor or dentist who is registered under the health services scheme. You have to pay part of the cost of some services, such as X-rays, physiotherapy and dentures.

Prescriptions

Ask at the local IKA for a list of pharmacists registered under the health services scheme. Take your prescription and health services book to one; you will be asked to pay a small standard charge plus 20 per cent of the cost of the medicines. If you have to pay the full cost, ask for a receipt and your prescription back, and keep the price-stickers from the medicine bottles and packets for your refund claim.

Hospital treatment

- If you are taken to hospital in an emergency, show your form E111 to the hospital administration, and ask them to get a hospital voucher for you from the IKA.

- If a doctor recommends hospital treatment, ask for a written statement and take it to an IKA office. They will issue a voucher, which will admit you to a hospital operating under the health services scheme.

- If you are treated in a private hospital for an emergency, you must pay the full cost. Ask for itemized receipts and take them within three days to an IKA office, with your health services book and your form E111. They will refund the amount allowed under the health services scheme.

- If there is no IKA office where you require treatment, pay for private treatment and medicines. Get receipts and apply for a refund once you return to the UK.

Social Insurance Institute (IKA)

IKA, 8 Aghiou Constantinou Street,
Athens

There are regional offices (*Ypokatastimata*) and local branches (*Parartimata*).

Refunds

Refunds will be granted in the situations above. You must show receipts perforated with a number. If you cannot obtain a refund abroad, keep receipts and drug price stickers for claiming in the UK.

ICELAND

Non-EEA nationals who are resident in the UK may be covered for emergency treatment in Iceland under a separate reciprocal arrangement. If so, you will need to show your NHS card.

Consulting a doctor or dentist

Go to a health centre and show your form E111. You will be charged a standard fee for medical treatment, and the full cost of dental treatment (children under age 16 pay 25 per cent of the cost of dental treatment). All charges are non-refundable.

Prescriptions

Take your prescription to a pharmacy. You will be charged a set amount, depending on the type of medicine. You can sometimes reduce the cost by requesting a generic rather than brand-name medicine.

Hospital treatment

- A doctor will refer you to hospital.
- In an emergency, you can be treated at the nearest public hospital.

- There is no charge for in-patient treatment.
- There is a set charge for out-patient treatment.

Information centre

For information, contact:

Ministry of Health and Social Security
(Tryggingastofnun Rikisins)
Laugavegi 116
IS-150 Reykjavik

Refunds

Refunds are not given for the standard fees charged for public treatment. If you think you have been wrongly charged for private treatment and wish to apply for a refund, present your receipts to the Ministry of Health and Social Security.

IRISH REPUBLIC

Consulting a doctor or dentist

Go to a local Health Board and ask them to arrange for you to see a doctor or dentist registered in the public health service. Tell the doctor or dentist that you want to be treated under EEA arrangements. Treatment should be free.

Prescriptions

Take your prescription to any dispensing chemist. There is normally no charge for most medicines.

Hospital treatment

- If you are taken to hospital in an emergency, ask to be treated under EEA arrangements.
- If a doctor recommends hospital treatment, ask to be admitted to a hospital operating under the public health service and to a free public ward.

Information centres

Local Health Boards have information on health service practitioners.

Refunds

Refunds do not apply as treatment is normally free.

ITALY

Consulting a doctor or dentist

- If you need to see a doctor or dentist urgently, you will have to pay and claim a refund later. Ask for itemized receipts, take them with your E111 to the local health unit – Unità Sanitaria Locale (USL) – and ask for a certificate of entitlement. Any refund given will probably only be partial.

- If possible, go to a local USL first and give them your form E111. Ask for a certificate of entitlement and for a list of doctors and dentists registered under the sickness insurance scheme. Take your certificate to any of the listed practitioners, who will charge you a fee.

Prescriptions

Take your prescription to a registered pharmacist. You will have to pay a fixed charge and part of the cost of each item prescribed. If you are charged the full price, ask for an itemized receipt, and keep the price tags on the bottles for your refund claim. If the receipt says 'ticket', the cost of the prescription is not refundable.

Hospital treatment

- If you are taken to hospital in an emergency, give form E111 to the hospital administration and ask them to contact the local USL immediately to request medical treatment.

- If a doctor recommends hospital treatment, he or she will give you a certificate (*proposta di ricovero*) entitling you to reduced-cost treatment in hospitals under the public health scheme. Have the certificate authorized by the local USL, and ask to see a list of local hospitals subscribing to the scheme.

Local health units

USLs are the local health units from which to get information and refunds. They can be found in all regions.

Refunds

If you do not obtain a certificate of entitlement before being treated (in a non-emergency), you may receive only a partial refund. If you cannot obtain a refund while abroad, keep your receipts and drug price stickers for claiming in the UK.

LUXEMBOURG

Consulting a doctor or dentist

Arrange to see a doctor or dentist and show form E111. Pay for the treatment and ask for an itemized receipt in order to claim a refund.

Prescriptions

Take your prescription to a dispensing chemist, pay for the medicines and ask for an itemized receipt.

Hospital treatment

- If you are taken to hospital in an emergency, show form E111 to the hospital administration and ask them to contact the local sickness fund office to arrange for treatment, which is normally free.

- If a doctor recommends hospital treatment, he or she will give you a certificate to give to the hospital administration entitling you to treatment, which is normally free. If you have not already visited a sickness fund office and handed over form E111, give it to the hospital administration. You will have to pay a daily charge for the time in hospital, which will not be refunded.

Sickness fund offices

> National Sickness Insurance Fund for Manual
>   Workers (Caisse nationale d'assurance-maladie
>   des ouvriers)
> 125 route d'Esch
> L-1471 Luxembourg Ville

Sickness fund offices can be found locally.

Refunds

Full and partial refunds are given.

NETHERLANDS

Consulting a doctor or dentist

- If you need to see a doctor or dentist urgently, give them a photocopy of your form E111. Medical treatment is usually free, but you may have to pay part of the cost of dental treatment.
- If possible, first go to the local sickness insurance fund and ask for a list of doctors who practise within the sickness insurance scheme. Visit during surgery hours, and give the doctor or dentist a copy of your E111.

Prescriptions

Give your prescription and a photocopy of form E111 to a dispensing chemist. You will have to pay a charge for each item on the prescription.

Hospital treatment

- If you are taken to hospital in an emergency, give a photocopy of form E111 to the hospital administration and ask them to obtain authorization for free treatment from the local sickness insurance fund office.
- If possible, see a doctor first and ask him or her to apply for authorization for free hospital in-patient treatment from the local sickness insurance fund office.

Sickness insurance fund offices

    Algemeen Nederlands Onderling Ziekenfonds (ANOZ), Kaap Hoorndreef 24-28, Utrecht

There are local offices in all areas.

NORWAY

Consulting a doctor or dentist

You should obtain treatment from a medical practitioner who is part of the National Insurance Administration (most are). If in doubt, consult the local sickness office.

- If consulting a doctor direct, you must show your form E111.
- You are required to pay a proportion of the costs of medical treatment, and the full cost of dental treatment.

Prescriptions

Take your prescription to a pharmacy. You will have to pay the full cost of all prescriptions except those given in hospital.

Hospital treatment

- A general practitioner will refer you to hospital. Your

admission must then be agreed by hospital doctors.
- In an emergency, you can be treated at the nearest public hospital.
- All hospital treatment is free.

Sickness offices

For information, contact a sickness office (*Lokale Trygdekontor*) for the area in which you are staying, or:

> National Insurance Administration
> (*Rikstrygdeverket*)
> Drammensveien 60
> Oslo 20, Norway

Refunds

No refunds apply.

PORTUGAL
(including the Azores and Madeira)

Consulting a doctor or dentist

- You can be treated at a health centre (*Centro de Saúde*), where you show your passport and ask to be treated under EEA arrangements. If you are not a UK national, show your form E111. You must pay a small charge.
- You will probably have to pay for dental treatment and you cannot claim a refund.
- In Madeira, if you have private medical treatment, you will have to pay. If you are charged, ask for the official green receipt and claim a small refund at the nearest appointed commercial bank (the health centres services will tell you which one).

Prescriptions

Take your prescription to a dispensing chemist and

show your passport. Some medicines prescribed for serious diseases are free of charge. You will be charged between 20 per cent and 60 per cent of the cost of others, and the full cost of some.

Hospital treatment

Show your passport (or E111 in the case of non-UK nationals) to the hospital administration and ask to be treated under EEA arrangements. You may have to pay for services such as laboratory tests and X-rays.

Regional Health Services offices

In Portugal, Regional Health Service offices – *Administração Regional de Saúde* – are found in all areas.

In the Azores, go to the Regional Health Service Directorate in Angra do Heroismo.

In Madeira, go to the Regional Health Directorate, Funchal.

Refunds

Refunds are limited and partial and do not apply for private treatment. Refunds of charges in Madeira must be claimed there.

SPAIN

Consulting a doctor or dentist

● Treatment under EEA arrangements is provided by doctors practising in the public health scheme. You can find health scheme doctors at their surgeries (*consultorio*), a health centre (*centro sanitario*) or hospital clinic (*ambulatorio*). Go during surgery hours and produce your form E111, giving the doctor a photocopy.

● If you need to see a doctor urgently, show form E111

and give the doctor a photocopy, explaining that you want to be treated under EEA arrangements. If you are charged, ask for an itemized receipt.

● Dental treatment is rarely available under the national health care scheme and you will have to pay for private treatment.

Prescriptions

Take your prescription to a dispensing chemist (*farmacia*). EEA pensioners are entitled to free medicines; everyone else must pay up to 40 per cent of the cost.

Hospital treatment

● If you are taken to hospital in an emergency, you will have to pay as a private patient unless you are admitted to a public ward in a state hospital. Show your E111 to the hospital authorities, give them a photocopy, and ask to be treated under EEA arrangements.

● If a doctor recommends hospital treatment, ask to be admitted to a public ward in a state hospital. Show Form E111 and give a photocopy to the hospital authorities as soon as you arrive.

Social Security Institute offices

Instituto Nacional de la Seguridad Social (INSS) has district offices (*dirección provincial*) throughout Spain. Other offices include the Catalan Health Service, the Basque Health Service, the Valencian Health Service, the Andalusian Health Service, and the National Institute for Health in other areas.

Refunds

Go to a Social Security Institute office, show them form E111 and give them a photocopy and receipts for any payments you have made, and ask for a refund. The cost of treatment as a private hospital patient will only be made, in Spain or the UK, if it was given in a life or death situation and no state hospital was available.

SWEDEN

Non-EEA nationals who are resident in the UK may be covered for emergency treatment in Sweden under a separate reciprocal arrangement. If so, you will need to show your NHS card.

Consulting a doctor or dentist

Obtain treatment from a medical practitioner who is part of the public insurance scheme. If in doubt, consult the local social insurance office.

- You must present form E111. You will be charged a standard fee, which is non-refundable.
- You will be charged about 50 per cent of the cost of dental treatment.

Prescriptions

Take your prescription to a pharmacy. You will be charged a standard fee.

Hospital treatment

- You can receive treatment in any public hospital emergency unit (*akutmottagningen*).
- You will be charged a proportion of the cost for out-patient care at a hospital.
- Hospital in-patient treatment is free.

Social insurance offices

For information, contact the social insurance office (*Lokala Forsakringskassan*) for the area in which you are staying.

Refunds

Refunds are not paid on the standard fees charged for

medical and dental treatment. The costs of private treatment are not refundable.

TREATMENT IN NON-EEA COUNTRIES WITH RECIPROCAL AGREEMENTS

The UK has reciprocal medical agreements with some 22 non-EEA member countries. Country-by-country details are listed on the following pages.

Bear in mind the following points:

- The arrangements for medical treatment vary considerably from country to country. In some they cover emergency treatment only, and in most you will have to make some payments. It is essential to arrange for medical insurance before leaving the UK to be sure you are fully covered.
- The treatment available may not be the same treatment you would expect to receive in an EEA country. In poorer countries medical facilities may not be adequate to deal fully with your condition, and the high-technology surgical facilities you would expect at home may not be available.
- In most cases you will need to show a valid UK passport. You may also have to show your UK National Health Service medical card or a driving licence.
- No refunds are available in the UK for costs incurred in non-EEA countries. In some countries you can obtain a full or partial refund for some services from a local health authority.

ANGUILLA

- Minor emergency treatment is usually free.

● You pay for ambulance services, out-patient and in-patient hospital care, dental treatment and prescribed medicines.

AUSTRALIA
● Hospital services are free.
● You pay for ambulance services, treatment by certain doctors (ask for a receipt), and prescribed medicines.
● For entitlement to free hospital services you must register with a local Medicare office before or after treatment. You can claim partial refunds of some doctors' charges from Medicare offices.

BARBADOS
● Ambulance services, medical treatment at polyclinics and hospitals, and prescribed medicines for children and elderly people are all free.
● You pay for dental treatment and, if you are not in an exempt category, prescribed medicines.

BRITISH VIRGIN ISLANDS
● Medical and hospital services are free for school-age children and over-70s.
● You pay full charges for all services if you are not in an exempt category.

BULGARIA
● Medical, hospital and dental services are free.
● You pay for medicines supplied by a public pharmacy.

CHANNEL ISLANDS
● Medical treatment is available for stays of up to three months.

On Guernsey/Alderney:
- All medical treatment (including in-patient hospital treatment, emergency dental treatment and ambulance travel) is free.
- There is no out-patient hospital treatment at Guernsey General Hospital.
- You pay for some prescribed medicines.

On Jersey:
- All hospital treatment and ambulance travel is free, as is treatment at the clinic of the General Hospital.
- You pay for treatment at a doctor's surgery, dental care and prescribed medicines.

On Sark:
- All medical treatment is free.
- Hospital care is provided on Guernsey.

CZECH REPUBLIC
- Medical and hospital services are free.
- You pay for prescribed medicines.

FALKLAND ISLANDS
- Ambulance services, medical, hospital and dental services, and prescribed medicines are free.

HONG KONG
- Emergency treatment at some hospitals and clinics is free. A list is available from: DH IRU, Richmond House, 79 Whitehall, London SW1A 2NS.
- You pay small charges for all other treatment and services.

HUNGARY
- Medical treatment in a doctor's surgery, a polyclinic or hospital is free.

- You pay for dental and ophthalmic treatment, and a standard charge for prescribed medicines.

ISLE OF MAN

- Medical and hospital treatment is as for the National Health Service in the UK.
- You pay for dental treatment and prescribed medicines.

MALTA

- Urgent medical treatment at area health centres, district dispensaries and state hospitals is free for visitors staying up to 30 days.
- You pay for private (non-goverment) medical treatment and prescribed medicines.

MONTSERRAT

- Medical treatment at government hospitals and clinics is free for over-65s and under-16s, and dental treatment is free for school children.
- You pay for ambulance services, medical and hospital treatment, dental treatment and most prescribed medicines.

NEW ZEALAND

- Dental treatment for under-19s and some prescribed medicines are free.
- You pay for medical and hospital treatment, and some medicines.
- Show your passport and ask community and hospital doctors whether you can claim a refund. If you are charged, ask for an itemized receipt, and claim a re-fund at a local health office. Contact the New Zealand Department of Health to request a cash benefit.

POLAND
- Medical, hospital and some dental treatment is free.
- You pay for a doctor's visit and 30 per cent of the cost of prescribed medicines from a public pharmacy.

ROMANIA
- Medical, hospital and some dental treatment are free.
- You pay for medicines from a public pharmacy.

SLOVAKIA
- Hospital and medical treatment are free.
- You pay for prescribed medicines.

ST HELENA
- Treatment in a hospital out-patient clinic during normal hours is free.
- You pay for ambulance services, hospital in-patient and dental treatment, and prescribed medicines.

TURKS AND CAICOS ISLANDS
- All medical services for under-16s and over-65s are free. Others are entitled to free ambulance services, dental treatment at clinics, and prescribed medicines on Grand Turk Island; and to medical treatment at government clinics and prescribed medicines on the Outer Islands.
- You pay for medical and hospital in-patient treatment on Grand Turk Island.
- There is no hospital on the Outer Islands.

FORMER USSR
(covering only the republics of Armenia, Azerbaijan, Belarus, Georgia, Kazakhstan, Kirgizstan, Moldova, Russia, Tajikistan, Turkmenistan, Uzbekistan, Ukraine)

- Medical, hospital and some dental treatment are free.
- You pay for prescribed medicines.

FORMER YUGOSLAVIA
(covering the republics of the former Yugoslavia: Serbia, Montenegro and successor states Croatia, Bosnia, Slovenia and Macedonia)

- Medical, hospital and some dental treatment is free.
- You pay for prescribed medicines.

TREATMENT IN OTHER COUNTRIES

Countries with which the UK has no reciprocal medical arrangements include some of the richest and the poorest: the USA and Canada, Mexico, Switzerland, most Caribbean islands, and the countries of Africa, the Middle East, Asia (except Hong Kong and some former Soviet republics), the Pacific region (except Australia and New Zealand) and South America.

If travelling to these countries, it is *essential* that you have comprehensive medical insurance with adequate coverage (see pp.26–7). Also, find out as much as you can about medical facilities (and costs, to help determine what level of insurance cover you need) in your destination country before you go by contacting its embassy in the UK.

Sources of information on doctors and other medical treatment include the following:

- If you are ill, telephone a UK consulate and ask for help in finding medical assistance.
- In countries where the UK has no diplomatic representation, the consulate of a country friendly to the UK (such as France or Sweden) may be willing to help with information and advice.

- Representatives of other organizations, such as The British Council and international aid agencies, may be able to give information.
- Hotels usually keep lists of doctors and dentists and can inform you about clinics, hospitals and pharmacies.
- Some airports have medical staff, and travel agents may know about medical services.
- If you are far from a town, try approaching a church or mission for help and information.

8. After you return

Many diseases have long incubation periods – that is, symptoms may not appear for weeks or even months after exposure (see pp.242–3). This can lead to diseases going undiagnosed once you return home; many of the common symptoms of dangerous diseases can be mistaken for flu or stomach upsets.

Even if you have no symptoms, you may want to undergo a health check on returning. This is particularly advisable if you've been in Africa, the Far East, southeast Asia or South America for longer than one month. Studies of large numbers of people who return to Britain after a spell in the tropics have shown that about 25 per cent of them have a detectable health abnormality. This is not to suggest that a quarter of returning travellers are ill or will become ill, but it does indicate that there is at least a case for considering whether a health check would be a good idea.

SELF-MONITORING

You must take responsibility for observing your state of health upon your return, and for alerting your doctor to any special concerns.

● If you decide not to have a routine health check when you return, be aware of any symptoms you experience. If you develop *any* form of illness within a month of returning, it is essential to tell your doctor that you have been abroad and where you have been. If, much later, you develop an unusual or medically puzzling illness, you must tell your doctors that you have been abroad. You should also make a point of referring to any activities or occupation you may have engaged in while abroad; it might be relevant to the condition.

● If you donate blood after returning, inform the staff if you travelled outside Europe or had treatment while abroad.

● If you have been taking a course of antimalarial drugs, remember to continue for one month after you return.

● If you received any treatment or medication while abroad, inform your doctor.

There are a number of symptoms you should be aware of if they arise; unexplained fever, chills, rashes, or diarrhoea may have ordinary causes, such as flu, but they can also be caused by serious diseases.

Unexplained fever
The most obvious indication that you might have come home incubating a tropical disease is an otherwise unexplained fever. A fever is defined as a rise in body temperature above the normal 37° C (98.6° F). Fevers have a variety of causes, the most common being bacterial or viral infection. Very high fever (41.5° C/104° F) must not be allowed to persist; it may result in brain damage.

If you have been travelling in a malarial area, malaria is a possibility, even if you have been taking antimalarial medication. The drugs are not 100 per cent reliable, although they are an essential preventive measure.

Other possible indications of malaria are:
- headache
- vomiting
- diarrhoea
- yellowing of the skin (jaundice)
- severe shivering
- abdominal pain
- cough
- malaise (a general feeling of being unwell)

None of these, however, is absolutely specific to malaria and may be caused by a number of other conditions you might have picked up in the tropics. If you have any of these symptoms after travelling in a malarial area, see a doctor immediately and give him or her details of where you have travelled.

Other conditions that may cause unexplained fever after returning from the tropics include:
- amoebiasis
- hepatitis
- pelvic infection
- tuberculosis
- urinary infection
- brucellosis
- leishmaniasis
- trypanosomiasis
- typhoid
- meningitis

Other symptoms

Any of the possible symptoms of malaria (as listed above) should be taken seriously and described to a doctor if you have been in a malarial area. Even if you have not been to a malaria-risk area, these and other – sometimes quite vague – symptoms can suggest a number of other serious conditions that require medical attention. They include:
- diarrhoea, especially if blood-stained
- vomiting
- tiredness
- rash
- itchiness

- swelling (of skin or glands)
- loss of appetite

MEDICAL EXAMINATIONS

If you develop any of the above symptoms after travelling and they cannot be attributed to a known cause, you should insist on a thorough medical examination. The doctor who examines you will be looking for the presence of any skin rashes and will check for lymph nodes that are swollen enough to be felt. He or she will also take particular care to check whether your liver and spleen have become enlarged. Enlargement of one or both of these organs is an important sign of several tropical diseases, especially malaria, leishmaniasis, hepatitis and amoebiasis. If you continue to feel well after returning from the tropics, you are unlikely to be suffering from any significant tropical disorder. Even so, a medical examination is the best way to rule out possible diseases if you have experienced symptoms, even if they seem to have cleared up. Some conditions have symptoms that disappear and reappear.

TESTS
Blood tests

Many tropical diseases can be detected by straightforward blood tests. Some of these diseases are caused by microscopic parasites that live in, or appear in, the blood. In these cases, a fine blood smear on a slide, examined under the microscope, can often detect these parasites and lead to a correct diagnosis. Among other diseases, malaria, filariasis and trypanosomiasis

INCUBATION PERIODS

Disease	Incubation period
AIDS	1–10 years
Cholera	1–3 days
Diphtheria	2–5 days
Gastroenteritis/ food poisoning	2–24 hours after a meal
German measles	14–21 days
Infective hepatitis	up to 3 months
Japanese encephalitis	unknown
Lassa fever	3–21 days
Legionnaires' disease	5–7 days
Leishmaniasis	1 month to 2 years
Lyme disease	3–30 days
Malaria	5 days to 1 year
Marburg disease	up to 1 week
Measles	8–12 days

Disease	Incubation period
Meningitis	2–14 days
Paratyphoid fever	2 weeks
Plague	2 days to 1 week
Poliomyelitis	7–14 days
Rabies	1–2 months
Sleeping sickness (trypanosomiasis)	5 days to 3 weeks
Smallpox	8–16 days
Tetanus	3–21 days
Trachoma	weeks or months
Tuberculosis	6 weeks
Typhoid fever	2 weeks
Worms (trichinosis, schistosomiasis, filariasis, etc.)	varies
Yellow fever	3–6 days

can be diagnosed positively in this way.

Blood tests are not confined to microscopy, however. A far wider range of conditions can be detected by blood tests because these conditions produce, in the blood, highly specific antibodies which can also be detected and identified.

In addition, checks of the levels of certain white blood cells can show whether or not you have picked up a worm infestation. Biochemical blood tests can also determine whether you have suffered any liver damage from hepatitis, amoebiasis or schistosomiasis.

Stool tests

Stool tests are not a pleasant thought, but could prove necessary if amoebic dysentery or amoebiasis is suspected. These tests can also show the cystic forms of various other tropical amoebic parasites. Most readily of all, they can show the larval forms of some parasitic worms and the eggs of several other worms, including:

- hookworms
- roundworms
- threadworms
- schistosome worms
- trichuria worms

Urine tests

Urine tests are mostly quick and very simple, and can be used to detect a variety of abnormalities such as kidney or liver damage, or the presence of parasitic or other important diseases of the urinary system. Sometimes these routine tests can be useful in revealing important conditions such as diabetes, quite unrelated to your stay abroad, but previously undetected.

Appendix: Helplines

There are a number of organizations in the UK that serve as important resources on travel health. Many offer their services free or at low cost. Refer to them for the most up-to-date information on vaccination requirements and disease risk areas.

General travel health information

● The **Department of Health** issues a valuable booklet called *Health Advice for Travellers*. You can pick up a copy in the post office or request one by phoning **0800 555 777** at no cost. Bulk copies can be obtained from BAPS, Health Publications Unit, Heywood Stotes, Manchester Road, Heywood, Lancs, OL10 2PZ.

Information on safety risks

● The **Foreign Office** will provide UK travellers with information on safety risks in foreign countries, such as terrorism and civil disturbances. Call **071 270 4129** or **4179** between 9:30am and 4pm.

Immunization: vaccines and information

● **Your GP** can provide you with some vaccinations, including diphtheria, polio and tetanus. For more specialized vaccines, you will need to attend a special travel health clinic listed below.

● **The Hospital for Tropical Diseases**, 4 St Pancras Way, London NW1 0PE, Tel. **071 388 9600** runs a travel clinic. The hours are Monday–Friday, 9–4:30, by appointment only. They provide a single consultation and written information tailored to your requirements. The £15 charge is waived if you buy your vaccines and drugs from them. They also sell useful items for travel, including repellents and chemicals, and they operate a Healthline on **0839 337733**. This service (which costs 49p/39p cheap rate per minute) will provide you with information on a particular country's health risks and requirements.

- **Medical Advisory Service for Travellers Abroad (MASTA)** runs a traveller's health line on **0891 224100.** This service, which costs the price of the phone call (49p/39p cheap rate per minute), will provide you with a print-out that meets your travel requirement. When you call, be ready to state:
  - where you are going and when
  - the type of accommodation in which you will be staying

  MASTA also sells useful items for travel, including the newly produced Mosi-guard insect repellent. This is an alternative to harsher DEET-based repellents, which have been known to damage plastic and may be harmful (see pp.76–7).

- The **London School of Hygiene and Tropical Medicine** has a malaria reference laboratory from which travellers can receive information on the malaria risk at their destination and on preventive measures. The 24-hour helpline is on **0891 600350** and costs the price of the phone call (49p/39p cheap rate per minute).

- **British Airways Travel Clinics** can be found in many parts of Britain. They provide travel advice and vaccinations, by appointment. Call **071 831 5333** to find the clinic nearest you.

TRAVEL HEALTH INFORMATION FOR DOCTORS ONLY

- The malaria reference laboratory at the London School of Hygiene and Tropical Medicine provides doctors with advice on malaria. For information on antimalarial treatment, call **071 636 7921** and ask to speak with a member of advisory staff in the malaria reference laboratory. For clinical information on particular cases, call **071 636 8636** and ask to speak with the duty medical officer.

Doctors can also get advice on travel health from:
- Department of Communicable and Tropical Diseases, Birmingham Hartlands Hospital, B9 5SS. Tel. **021 766 6611**.
- Department of Infectious Diseases and Tropical Medicine, North Manchester Health Care Trust, Delaunays Road, Crumpsall, Manchester M8 6RB. Tel **061 795 4567**.
- Liverpool School of Tropical Diseases, Pembroke Place, Liverpool L3 5QA. Tel. **051 708 9393**.

Index

COLLINS GEM

GEMS TO PACK

Choose from a selection of Gems that cater for both the practical and fun sides of a holiday.

Gem First Aid £3.50

A practical, clear guide to first aid treatment for both life-threatening conditions and common, everyday ailments and injuries.

Gem SAS Survival Guide £3.99

If you are off the beaten track, this guide shows you how to survive. Includes information on what to eat, first aid and navigating.

Gem Holiday Games £3.50

Contains a varied selection of indoor and outdoor games requiring only simple equipment or none at all.

Gem Card Games £3.50

A compact guide to over 100 popular family card games.

Gem Children's Games £3.50

Includes ball games, singing games, dominoes, tiddlywinks and word games.

Gem Travel Games £3.50

A unique compendium of observation games, word and guessing games, paper and pencil games, and things to make and do.

LANGUAGE GEMS

Gem Phrase Finders are designed for ease of use. The 2-colour design ensures that key words, essential information, and the foreign phrases are immediately accessible. Over 70 topics are listed alphabetically. The flexible phrases can be tailored to suit individual situations. A simple pronunciation guide allows you to reproduce the right sounds without being daunted by foreign spelling. A mini-dictionary provides a practical selection of vocabulary.

DUTCH £3.50

FRENCH £2.99

GERMAN £2.99

GREEK £2.99

ITALIAN £2.99

PORTUGUESE £2.99

SPANISH £2.99

COLLINS GEM

Bestselling Collins Gem titles include:

Gem English Dictionary (£3.50)

Gem Calorie Counter (£2.99)

Gem Thesaurus (£2.99)

Gem French Dictionary (£3.50)

Gem German Dictionary (£3.50)

Gem Burns Anthology (£3.50)

Gem Birds (£3.50)

Gem Babies' Names (£3.50)

Gem Card Games (£3.50)

Gem World Atlas (£3.50)